HOW TO BUILD KITCHEN CABINETS, COUNTERS AND VANITIES

HOW TO BUILD KITCHEN CABINETS, COUNTERS AND VANITIES

Don Geary

Reston Publishing Company, Inc.
A Prentice-Hall Company
Reston, Virginia

Library of Congress Cataloging in Publication Data

Geary, Don.
  How to build kitchen cabinets, counters and vanities.

  Includes index.
  1. Cabinet-work. I. Title.
TT197.G42   749'.3   78-10312
ISBN 0-8359-2933-7

© 1979 by Reston Publishing Company, Inc.
A Prentice-Hall Company
Reston, Virginia 22090

10 9 8 7 6 5 4 3 2 1

Printed in the United States of America

CONTENTS

INTRODUCTION

It is apparent that the costs of building or maintaining a home will never go down; in fact it almost seems that in the future owning a home will be a privilege of the well-to-do. Part of the reason for the astronomical cost is directly related to the higher prices for construction materials—the cost for a single sheet of one-half-inch-thick, four-by-eight-foot plywood has tripled over the past year. It seems safe to say that the prices of building materials in general will continue to rise in the future.

Another very large part of the cost of modern building is the labor involved. Skilled carpenters receive (depending on factors such as location and union scale) between eight and fifteen dollars an hour in wages. Overall costs for construction are approximately one-third for materials and two-thirds for labor. Obviously if part or all of the actual labor can be accomplished by the homeowner, the overall cost of a building project will be considerably lower than if the same project were to be done by a professional.

Probably the biggest deterrent for homeowners in building projects is lack of information; another is inexperience in working with hand or power tools. The purpose of this book is to help provide the necessary information for building kitchen cabinets, counters and bathroom vanities. Your proficiency with tools can, of course, only come with actual work. Basic but helpful information about modern hand tool use will be found in Chapter 1.

It is important to keep in mind that almost anything can be constructed by the do-it-yourselfer providing that he or she has a well-thought-out work plan. Planning is the key to predictable results and cannot be overemphasized. The amount of time you devote to planning will be directly related to the final results of the cabinet building project. During the planning stages, you should consult as many sources as possible to see not only the various designs available but how different types of cabinets are put together. There are many magazines devoted to decorating the home (*Better Homes and Gardens, American Home* and *House Beautiful* are just a few). Some issues of these magazines are devoted to specific areas of the home, such as the kitchen or bathroom. It will be helpful to you, during your planning stages, to consult these periodicals for design and practical ideas.

Another helpful aid during the planning stage is to visit home improvement centers, cabinet shops and even friends' homes to see how cabinets, counters and vanities are constructed. Looking at cabinets that are already constructed will give you a real insight into how to go about building your own. Be curious and you will see how other builders accomplished the same things you are about to try. Chapter 2 goes into greater detail about planning, including information about how to draw up a work plan that can and should be used during your actual building. Devote enough time to your work plan so that you will have a clear understanding of how the various building tasks are to be accomplished. Then use this plan as you work. By working in this fashion you will have an edge on the professional.

Other chapters in this book are designed to help you through the actual construction of cabinets, counters and vanities. Each of these chapters covers a major step in the building process such as: counter bases (which are similar for both kitchen counters and bathroom vanities), counter tops, plastic laminates, drawers, hardware, finishing and installation. Before beginning the actual construction, you should have read the entire book. Then as you proceed through the actual building, you should consult the text as often as necessary to help you through the building.

No book is possible without the help of others and this book is certainly no exception. In particular I would like to thank the American Plywood Association for the help they gave in providing photographs and information. I would also like to thank John Beck, who was kind enough to help with many of the photographs in this book. My wife, Virginia, was quite helpful in the final typing and understanding enough to offer encouragement when needed.

CHAPTER 1

TOOLS AND
MATERIALS

The modern do-it-yourselfer should be familiar with a variety of hand tools and machines. A knowledge of hand tools will make projects easier to accomplish and help in obtaining professional looking, as well as functioning, results. This first chapter will talk about the tools that are important to the home craftsman. Your ability to effectively use woodworking tools can come only as a result of actual work experience.

SAWS

Chances are very good that you already own at least one saw, either hand-held electric or a stationary electric, such as a bench or radial saw. Since most of the projects in this book utilize plywood, in one form or another, and involve long cuts—at least 2

1

feet—a table saw will be very useful providing, of course, you already own one and are familiar with its operation.

For all practical purposes you can make most of your cuts with a hand-held circular saw, with a blade size of about 7¼ inches. One of the benefits of using a hand-held circular saw (often referred to as a 'skill saw') is that it is portable. Straight as well as long cuts are not only possible but a simple operation once you become familiar with the saw. There are several attachments and guidance systems you can use to insure that the saw cuts exactly where you want it to.

There are quite a number of skill saws for sale, with a price range starting at under 20 dollars and topping off at about 75 dollars. It is safe to say that if you purchase one of the less expensive models you will not find it to be as accurate or long lasting as one in the 50 dollar price range. If you can afford to spend this much—a worthwhile investment for any serious woodworker—you should buy a saw commonly referred to as a 'contractor's saw'. This designation indicates that the saw has a horsepower rating of 1½-2 horse, and is built to take a little abuse. You will also find that most contractor's saws come with attachments, e.g., a ripping guide, which can make some work easier to accomplish. In addition, this type of saw can be easily adjusted for depth of cut or bevel cuts (Figure 1-1).

When you purchase a skill saw it will usually come with a saw blade attached. The blade that comes with your saw will, in all likelihood, be a combination blade which is suitable for most types of cutting. It will be to your advantage, however, to consider buying additional blades of different types before undertaking a cabinet or counter building project.

One blade that is worth the investment is a plywood blade. A blade of this type will enable you to make smooth cuts in plywood—the most common material used to build cabinets.

Another blade, carbide tipped, while easily twice the price of other types of blades, is also a worthwhile investment because it will hold an edge longer than any other material. Carbide tipped blades will also make clean cuts in plywood, plastic laminates, particle board, and other materials commonly used in cabinet making.

As the chart below (Figure 1-2) shows, there are several other types of blades for hand-held saws, and it is important that the proper blade is used for the type of work you are doing. One important point to keep in mind when using any type of saw blade is that a less than sharp blade will be hard to use. It will burn the

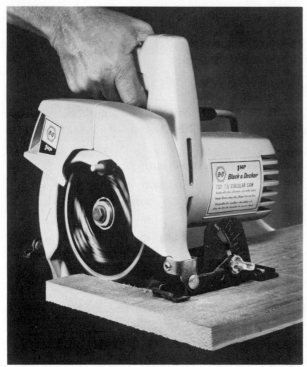

(Courtesy of Black & Decker)

Figure 1-1: Many woodworking projects can be quickly and easily accomplished using a hand-held circular saw such as this one.

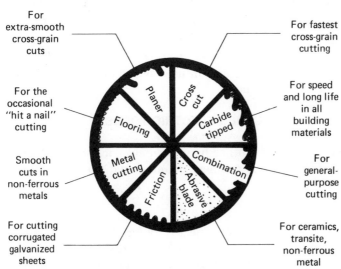

For extra-smooth cross-grain cuts

For the occasional "hit a nail" cutting

Smooth cuts in non-ferrous metals

For cutting corrugated galvanized sheets

For fastest cross-grain cutting

For speed and long life in all building materials

For general-purpose cutting

For ceramics, transite, non-ferrous metal

Planer

Cross cut

Flooring

Carbide tipped

Metal cutting

Combination

Friction

Abrasive blade

Figure 1-2: It is important to choose the right type of saw blade for the particular material being cut.

wood and be hard to push through the work. In addition, an unsharp blade is a safety hazard.

Safety Tips

Speaking of safety, there are a few simple rules that should always be followed when using any type of electric saw. The rules are:

- Always wear eye protection.
- Support the work properly to prevent the saw from binding. Improperly supported work can lead to saw bucking or throwing.
- Do not force the saw, let it cut at it's own speed. Forcing will cause the motor of the saw to overwork and this could lead to internal damage.
- Unplug the saw before changing blades.
- Make certain the switch is in the 'OFF' position before plugging in the saw.
- Keep both hands on the saw. If this is not practical keep the free hand well away from the blade.
- Do not cut short pieces of lumber with a hand-held saw.
- Be careful when cutting through knots—these may cause the saw to buck or kick back.
- When working with an electric saw (or any tool for that matter) keep your mind on the work, and do not try to do two things at once, such as carry on a conversation.
- Never operate a saw in need of repair or one that is not properly grounded.

OTHER ELECTRIC TOOLS

There are a few other hand-held electrical tools which you may need for building cabinets, counters and vanities. These are discussed briefly below.

Router

This very handy tool is necessary for all types of work with plastic laminates. Basically, a router consists of a high speed motor (about 25,000 rpm), a chuck for holding the cutting bit, and an adjustable base. Routers are hand-held, except that a radial arm saw often has a router chuck on one side of the motor. There are many different types of cutting bits for routers, as Figure 1-3

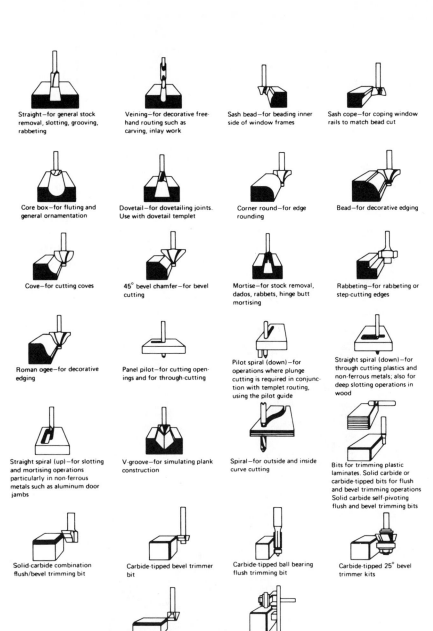

Straight—for general stock removal, slotting, grooving, rabbeting

Veining—for decorative free-hand routing such as carving, inlay work

Sash bead—for beading inner side of window frames

Sash cope—for coping window rails to match bead cut

Core box—for fluting and general ornamentation

Dovetail—for dovetailing joints. Use with dovetail templet

Corner round—for edge rounding

Bead—for decorative edging

Cove—for cutting coves

45° bevel chamfer—for bevel cutting

Mortise—for stock removal, dados, rabbets, hinge butt mortising

Rabbeting—for rabbeting or step-cutting edges

Roman ogee—for decorative edging

Panel pilot—for cutting openings and for through-cutting

Pilot spiral (down)—for operations where plunge cutting is required in conjunction with templet routing, using the pilot guide

Straight spiral (down)—for through cutting plastics and non-ferrous metals; also for deep slotting operations in wood

Straight spiral (up)—for slotting and mortising operations particularly in non-ferrous metals such as aluminum door jambs

V-groove—for simulating plank construction

Spiral—for outside and inside curve cutting

Bits for trimming plastic laminates. Solid carbide or carbide-tipped bits for flush and bevel trimming operations Solid carbide self-pivoting flush and bevel trimming bits

Solid-carbide combination flush/bevel trimming bit

Carbide-tipped bevel trimmer bit

Carbide-tipped ball bearing flush trimming bit

Carbide-tipped 25° bevel trimmer kits

Carbide-tipped combination flush/bevel trimming bit

Carbide-tipped 15° backsplash trimmer—with $\frac{5}{16}$″ diameter hole

Figure 1-3: There are many different types of router bits which will help you to add professional looking finishing touches.

5

shows. Some cutting bits have pilot bearings for guiding the cutter around the edge of the work while other bits do not. With the latter some type of guidance system must be used to keep the router in position during use.

Sabre Saw

A sabre saw is used for a variety of cutting jobs. The blade (there are many different types) is the reciprocating type (up and down) and cuts on the upstroke. A sabre saw is invaluable for making curved cuts. Special purpose blades of various lengths are available including blades for cutting wood, metal, plastic and other materials. Use the finest tooth blade possible to get a smooth, even cut. All of the better made sabre saws have a tilting base so bevel cuts can be made. While the sabre saw is undoubtedly the safest of the hand-held electric saws, the same safety rules for hand-held circular saws should be followed during operation (Figure 1-4).

(Courtesy of Black & Decker)

Figure 1-4:   A sabre saw is one of the safest electrical saws to use and it is capable of making many different types of cuts.

Sanders

There are two types of sanders: belt and disk sanders, and finish sanders. Belt or disk sanders require a bit of skill to use properly as they are fast cutting. These types must be kept moving continuously and never held in one spot. Each stroke of the sander should overlap the previous stroke by about one-half belt width. The weight of the machine provides just about the right amount of pressure to do the sanding, so you should never press the sander down into the work as this will put excess strain on the motor. There are basically three types of belts or sanding disks for these types of sanders: coarse, medium and fine.

Finish sanders are used when only a very slight amount of sanding is necessary because they remove very little of the surface. Generally speaking, finish sanders are driven either in an orbital or oscillating motion. Orbital sanders can be moved in any direction over the surface of the work while oscillating sanders work best when moved with the grain of the wood being sanded (Figure 1-5).

Drill

The portable electric drill is one common tool that most homeowners already own. While a drill is most often used for boring holes, it can also be used for grinding, sanding, and cutting

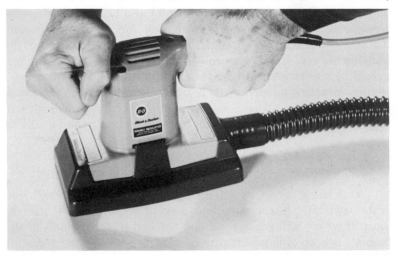

(Courtesy of Black & Decker)

Figure 1-5: A finish sander can be used to good advantage just prior to applying the finish coating.

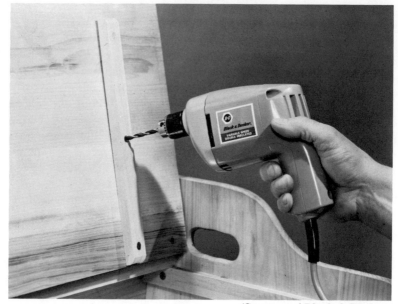

(Courtesy of Black & Decker)

Figure 1-6: An electric drill has many uses when building cabinets, counters and vanities.

when fitted with special accessory attachments. An electric drill with a variable speed motor (reversible) and fitted with a special screw driver attachment is very handy for driving or removing screws. The most popular drill sizes are ¼, ⅜ inch for the homeowner and ½ inch for professionals. Drill size is easily determined by the largest size drill shank the drill chuck will accept. Before operating an electric drill, tighten the drill bit in the chuck with a special key. Also keep in mind that a sharp drill bit will help you to accomplish work much more efficiently than a dull bit (Figure 1-6).

Shop Vacuum

One thing is certain when working with wood, you will generate sawdust, plaster dust, and piles of other waste materials, most of which will get carried and tracked to other parts of the home. To keep this problem in hand it is wise to consider some type of vacuum cleaner to clean up as you go along. You could, of course, use an ordinary household vacuum cleaner but these are usually not very efficient for picking up wood shavings, chips and piles of sawdust. It may be to your advantage to consider purchasing a vacuum cleaner designed for picking up these types of debris.

Personally, I prefer a portable type shop vacuum cleaner but I know several do-it-yourselfers who have installed a centrally located vacuum system (throughout the house) that is capable of accomplishing the cleanup task just as well. If you are planning to purchase a shop vacuum cleaner, give special consideration to the models that are capable of picking up both dry and wet materials. There are many types of shop vacuum cleaners to choose from as most of the electric tool manufacturers—Sears Roebuck, Black & Decker, Stanley—now sell them.

NONELECTRIC HAND TOOLS

While there are many different types of electric powered hand tools that can make a project go quicker, prices for these tools are often prohibitive for the average do-it-yourselfer and, therefore, most of your work will be done with simple hand tools (or possibly rented power equipment). I will briefly discuss the tools which are important for home building of cabinets, counters, and vanities.

Ruler

Two types of rulers are handy; a folding ruler (8-foot) and a steel tape with a length of about 25 feet. A ruler will save you time and money if you use it in conjunction with the old-time carpenter's rule: "Measure twice, cut once."

Hammer

It is safe to say that all of your home building projects can be accomplished with a 16-ounce hammer. It is interesting to note, however, that most professional builders use a 20-ounce hammer for all of their work. An important point to keep in mind about hammers is how it feels to you. A hammer which is too heavy will fatigue the user quickly. Another point to consider is that a lot of the fastening done when building cabinets, counters and vanities is done with adhesives and clamps, or screws rather than with a hammer and nails. One useful hammer accessory is a hammer holster or holder. With a holster strapped to your side, your hammer is always handy and ready for use.

Nail Set

A nail set is used for driving the heads of nails below the surface of the work. This is a necessary finishing touch for many cabinet designs.

Chalk Line

A chalk line is a simple tool which is a real aid in laying out work and for marking sheets of plywood for cutting. The real advantage of a chalk line is that you can mark a straight line over almost any surface quickly and easily.

Marking Gauge

A marking gauge is used for marking lumber along a line which is parallel to the edge of the board. It has a sliding head which can be moved along the length of the tool and locked into a stationary position with a set screw. A marking gauge is very handy for marking long cuts of under 6 inches and for marking lumber before making many of the woodworking joints used in this book (Figure 1-7).

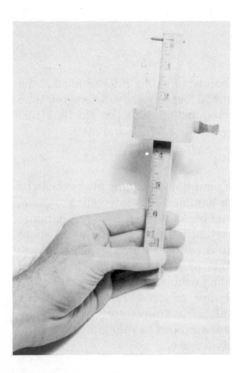

Figure 1-7: The marking gauge is designed to help you make accurate lines parallel to the edge of a board.

Clamps

Since much of cabinet, counter and vanity building involves the use of adhesives, an assortment of clamps is not only a good idea, but a necessity. There are many types of clamps: bar clamps, parallel clamps, spring clamps, C clamps, are just a few. Most of the projects in this book can be done with C and bar clamps however.

Screwdrivers

Screw driving and removing is not any easy task but the work will go much smoother if you use the proper size and length screwdriver for the type of screws you are working with. Use the longest screwdriver convenient for the job. The tip of the screwdriver should fit the screw slot snuggly, the tip should be square and no wider than the slot in the screw. A good selection of screwdrivers, both standard and Phillips, will help you to drive and remove screws with less effort.

Socket Set

Often there will be some part of a cabinet, counter or vanity that needs to be bolted, e.g., a wall installation. A complete set of sockets, ⅜-inch drive, with extension, will help you to tighten bolts with ease and efficiency.

Files and Rasps

You should have an assortment of files and rasps in your home tool box, and be familiar with their use. You should have at least two types: an 8-inch or 10-inch mill bastard file and a Stanley "Surform" tool. The bastard file will be necessary for finishing off the edges when working with plastic laminates and veneers. The "Surform" tool differs from a standard rasp in that it is essentially nonclogging. A file will be easier to use if it has a wooden or plastic handle. Clean the grooves with a file card after each use.

Adhesives

As mentioned earlier, much of cabinet, counter or vanity building is done with some type of adhesive, and in most cases this adhesive is white glue. One popular white glue that is used almost universally is Elmer's Glue-All. The key to white glues is that they have a water base, which means that they have a setup time that is longer than an epoxy or synthetic glue. Clamping is necessary with all white glues. Water-base glues are very safe to use, they contain no toxic solvents, they are safe to breathe and they won't ignite if exposed to an open flame. Another advantage of white glues is that your tools are easily cleaned with soap and water after use.

Another type of glue that is commanly used in counter making is contact cement. This is also a water-base adhesive but with a quicker setup time than standard white glue. It is interesting to note that some types of contact cements are not water-based but solvent based adhesives. Check the label before you purchase if you want a nontoxic contact cement. Solvent base adhesives will have a caution that the glue should be used with adequate ventilation and will ignite if exposed to an open flame. Water-based contact cements work as well as solvent based adhesives but without any health risks. (See Chapter 6 for more information about adhesives.)

Nails, Screws and Other Fasteners

These are all used in cabinet, counter and vanity building. For most purposes you will be using finishing nails (or casing nails, which hold better) when an operation calls for nailing. Finishing nails are made of finer wire than common nails and have smaller heads. A casing nail is similar to a finishing nail except it has a conical head. Both types are used in finishing work since their heads can be sunk below the surface (with a nail set) and the resultant hole filled with a suitable filler material.

Screws have greater holding power than nails, and therefore are a better choice when joining two pieces of wood that will be subject to stress and strain. Screws cost more than nails and require more time to drive (or remove) but the added strength they provide make them the only choice for many fastening jobs. Screws are made from steel, aluminum, brass, copper, and other materials. Choose the proper size and head style for the particular task at hand. Screw heads can be flat, round, oval or pan. Usually the flat and oval headed screws are countersunk, while the round and pan head screws are not. Before driving a screw it is necessary first to drill a hole (of proper and predetermined depth and diameter). Drill bits are available that will drill a hole and at the same time make it possible to countersink the screw (see Figure 1-8).

Bolts, masonry fasteners and anchor bolts are commonly used when installing cabinets to interior walls. There are several types including toggle bolts, "mollys" and others (see Chapter 10).

Figure 1-8: Several types of screws can be used in cabinet building. Some examples are (l. to r.): countersunk, round head, sheet metal, and the large screw along the bottom is a lag bolt.

Corrugated fasteners are a form of nail that is commonly used by professional cabinetmakers. Simply a piece of corrugated steel, with a sharpened bottom edge, these nails are used to join two pieces of wood, quickly and easily, where otherwise it would require a bit of difficult work, mitering joints for example.

WOOD JOINTS

Several different types of wood joints are used in cabinet making so it is to your advantage to learn how to make them. Important wood joints include: butt joints, lap joints (half, cross, end and middle lap joints), rabbet, dado, dovetail, miter, mortise, and tenon joints. Figure 1-9 shows these and combinations of these joints. A brief discussion of each of these joints follows:

Butt Joints

These are the simplest of all joints to make because two pieces of wood are placed together, glued, and then often nailed or clamped. The butt end joint should be square and the face surface should be smooth.

Lap Joints

For lap joints two pieces of wood are jointed in such a way as to equal the thickness of one piece. This is most easily accomplished by removing one half the thickness of each piece (opposing sides), gluing and then nailing or screwing. Lap joints are easily made on a table saw, or with a router. The key to making good lap joints is to measure carefully, as this will insure a tight and flush fit.

Rabbet and Dado Joints

These two joints are similar except that the rabbet is used at the edge of a piece of wood, while the dado is cut anywhere away

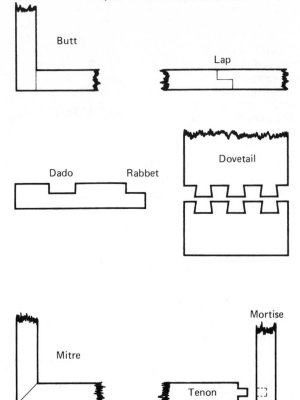

Figure 1-9:   Some of the woodworking joints used in cabinet building.

from the edges. Both of these joints are easy to make using either a table saw or router. Careful measuring and setup are the keys to success here.

Dovetail Joints

Dovetail joints are used in the construction of quality drawers. They are difficult to make by hand therefore you should consider using a simpler method which entails the use of a router and a special template. The router and template setup will enable you to produce really professional dovetail joints with just a little practice.

Miter Joints

Miter joints are used when two pieces of wood are to be joined at right angles and where edge appearance is important.

Miter joints are actually butt joints with the angle at the corner shared equally between the two pieces. In a right-angle miter, both pieces of wood are cut at an angle of 45 degrees and the resultant joint is equal to 90 degrees. A miter box will be helpful as a guide for cutting this type of joint. There are also attachments for table, or radial arm saws which will enable you to make this joint with ease.

Mortise and Tenon Joints

This joint is best explained as having male/female parts; the male being the tenon and the female being the mortise. Careful measuring and cutting is the key to this tight joint. A marking gauge is invaluable when marking the lumber for this type of joint. A sharp chisel is also necessary for this joint.

To be sure, there are other types of joints used in cabinet making, but most are just variations of those listed above. To make really strong joints, it is important that you measure carefully and cut with as much precision as possible. Joints will have even greater strength if glued and nailed or, better yet, glued and screwed. A more thorough discussion of woodworking joints can be found in Chapter 7.

Using the tools described in this chapter you will be able to construct your own kitchen cabinets, counters and bathroom vanities. The tools alone, however, are only an aid to performing certain tasks and will not make up for poor planning or sloppy work. A well-thought-out work plan and a conscientious approach are the best insurance for professional looking and functioning results.

CHAPTER 2

PLANNING

One of the most important parts of any remodeling project is the planning stage. It is during this stage that you must decide how you want the finished project to look and function. The most effective kind of planning takes into consideration every possible detail of the project. Think about your ability to work with hand tools; will you have to purchase additional tools or can you work effectively with the tools you presently own? Think also about finances; will you be able to purchase the necessary materials from available funds or will some type of outside financing be necessary? Another consideration is how much time can you devote to a remodeling project. A professional contractor can usually remodel an entire kitchen within one week but it may take you twice (or three times) as long to do the same work (see Figure 2-1).

(Courtesy of Tile Council of America)

Figure 2-1:   This kitchen was designed to be convenient to work in as well as attractive.

There are also other considerations. If you have never re-modeled a kitchen before there will undoubtedly be certain tasks which must be accomplished, but that you are not really qualified to perform, e.g., rewiring or other electrical work, plumbing (if you move the sink or dishwasher you will have to move the water and waste lines as well), roof raising, eliminating or adding an interior wall or installing a sliding glass door.

Although it is true that most people can accomplish what they set out to do, the fact remains that you may save yourself a lot of time, money and aggravation if you call in a professional to do some of the work.

In most cases the main reason for a remodeling project is to gain more efficiency from the area being remodeled. Kitchens are a prime example of this, especially in older houses; the cabinets may be too small, or too low or high; there may not be enough counter and work space; the refrigerator may be in one part of the kitchen, the stove in another and the sink in a third area. All is very inefficiently laid out which results in more time than is necessary to perform kitchen duties. A well thought out and constructed kitchen could save a lot of time—time that can be used for other interests.

Another reason for a remodeling project is to modernize. Older homes are again a prime target, not only because older kitchens may be inefficient, but because they may look as if they have been through some rough experiences. Old cabinets usually don't work well, and are often covered with several layers of chipping paint. The sink may be chipped, the faucet may leak and the floor may sag in the middle. Remodeling can breath new life into your kitchen and not only make it more efficient but also an attractive focal point in your home. The best way to approach remodeling—so you will be able to achieve predictable as well as professional looking results—is to plan thoroughly and thoughtfully.

The first step in the planning stage is to make a list of all the features you would like to have in your finished kitchen. The list may include: a wall oven, microwave oven, storage space that is easy to reach, a double sink (or triple sink), a faucet with a single lever control, a refrigerator, freezer, trash compactor, range top cooking unit, griddle, lots of counter and work space, an area for cookbooks and meal planning (a good location for the telephone), electrical outlets in convenient places, a waste disposal unit in the sink drain, dishwasher, effective lighting, etc. (see Figure 2-2).

After you have made as complete a list as possible, go through the list and cross out the inevitable frivolous items; do you really need three ovens and twelve burners? One real aid in the paring process is price, or how much you can afford to spend. That range top with built-in shishkebab brazier is nice but 300 dollars is a lot to spend for something which will get only occasional use. Obviously, you will be limited to some extent by costs, but some appliances or gadgets are a good investment; a pilot lightless stove can save you a few dollars every year, and is required in some states as an energy saving measure (see Figure 2-3).

Also think about the future, based on what you have read, as well as your past experiences. What is the best form of energy for your area—electric, gas or oil? During the planning stages of the remodeling project think about making a switch to the most eco-

(Courtesy of Jenn-Air Corporation)

Figure 2-2: A kitchen island with a built-in stove may make your kitchen more efficient. This unit has a special grill.

(Courtesy of Jenn-Air Corporation)

Figure 2-3: If you do a lot of baking two wall mounted ovens like these may save you a lot of kitchen time.

nomical form of energy. A check into local building codes is also a good idea and may in fact save some future headaches.

The next step, after you have decided what additions you can afford, is to draw a diagram of the project. Begin by measuring from wall to wall to wall. Transfer your measurements onto a piece of graph paper. Let each square on the paper equal six inches or one foot. Outline the area being remodeled on the graph paper eliminating all existing cabinets, counters and appliances. Include windows, doors, plumbing, electrical outlets, exhaust fans, heat registers (or air conditioning units) and anything else that is more or less permanent in the present room.

Now, while looking at the diagram, think about how you can make the new kitchen as functional and efficient as possible.Where, for example, would be the best location for the sink, stove, oven, refrigerator? Major appliances get first consideration because you will be limited to a certain extent as to where they can be located. Draw the location of these to scale on the graph paper.

Next, think about work space and storage. Where is the best place to store cooking utensils, canned goods, dinnerware, glassware? The location of storage and work areas should then be indicated on the graph paper (Figure 2-4).

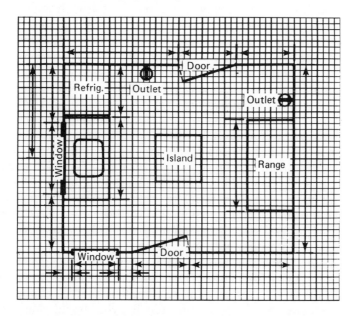

Figure 2-4: Plan your new kitchen on graph paper. Draw to scale all appliances, cabinets, counter space and other storage space.

Think also about existing windows and doors. Would moving the doorway six feet in one direction give you more usable space in the new kitchen? Would more windows, or relocating the existing ones give the new kitchen more light or make it more functional? Can you do renovations of this type or will you have to call in a professional?

Planning the right type of counters and cabinets is as important as their location. It is very convenient, for example, to have a cabinet close to the stove and oven. This cabinet can hold the most frequently used cooking utensils, pots, baking pans and other items. Another good idea for around the stove is some type of storage for spices and other ingredients that are used often in cooking.

One important aspect of kitchen planning to take into consideration is the person who will be using the kitchen the most. If you, as home remodeler also work in the kitchen, you will have a good idea of what types of counters and storage cabinets are needed. If, on the other hand, you are more likely to be found in the woodworking shop than at the kitchen counter, it would make a lot of sense to sit down and thoroughly plan the project with the main user, namely your spouse. Cabinet and counter height would be one such consideration (Figure 2-5).

Since this book can really only concern itself with the building of cabinets, counters and vanities, you will have to look elsewhere for more information about major kitchen and bathroom renovations. There are quite a number of magazines and periodicals that deal almost exclusively with these areas of the home. Some examples are: *American Home, Better Homes & Gardens, House Beautiful, The American Builder, How-To,* and *Workbench*. You may find it helpful to look through several back issues of these magazines for ideas. Keep in mind that these magazines will often have an entire issue devoted to the kitchen or bathroom and there will be quite a bit of current, useful information about storage units, appliances and other related items. But note, however, that most of the material in these magazines is for the homeowner who is planning to purchase ready-made storage units and have a professional do the installation. Still, magazines provide the do-it-yourselfer with worthwhile ideas.

Counter space in the kitchen is necessary and, generally speaking, the more the better. Think for a minute about all of the operations that are performed in the kitchen; mixing, chopping, cutting, and cleaning are just a few. Ideally, you should plan your kitchen so that there are areas where specific functions can be ac-

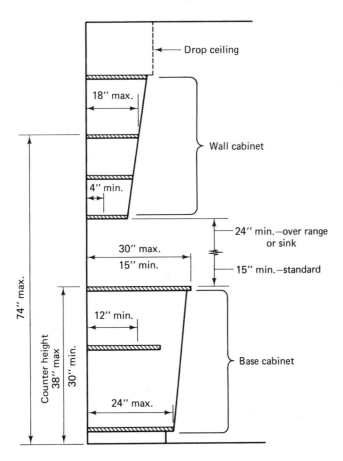

Figure 2-5: When planning your new kitchen it is important to consider the heights of counters and cabinets. Use the above diagram as a general guide.

complished. If you or your spouse do a lot of baking, it may be a good idea to have a section of the kitchen devoted to this particular function. This would mean a counter space that can be used for mixing ingredients, large enough for kneading dough, letting breads rise, and finally letting baked items cool undisturbed. A storage unit for baking ingredients and utensils would also be handy in this area.

Cutting, chopping, grating and other food preparation tasks are best accomplished on some type of cutting surface. Many modern kitchens use plastic laminate surfaces throughout the kitchen. This makes good sense as counter tops covered with plastic laminate are easy to keep clean, resist heat, do not generally stain, and provide a hard surface on which to work. To add a bit of functional warmth to your kitchen counters, consider building a butcher block type counter out of hardwood for one area of the kitchen—next to the kitchen sink is a good location.

Americans are big users of canned and frozen foods, therefore it makes sense to include some type of storage system that takes this fact into consideration. Consider a freezer for your kitchen. The chest type will usually hold more than an upright freezer, but the chest type also takes up more horizontal space. Think about building some type of revolving shelf (or several vertical shelves which fold together for compactness) for your canned goods. Simple additions such as these can make your kitchen more efficient, which means less time in the kitchen.

You will also need drawers in the kitchen for storing eating and cooking utensils—silverware, wooden spoons, spatulas, large forks and spoons, etc.

It might be convenient if you had one cabinet for housing all of your electrical appliances—blender, food processor, electric coffee maker, mixer, waffle iron and other items. To make a cabinet of this type even more efficient consider adding a drawer which can hold electrical cords for the appliances as well as related attachments.

Remember that the smaller the living space a family occupies, the more essential it becomes to use space to the fullest advantage. As I mentioned, it makes sound planning sense to have specific areas for storage and work, providing, of course, you have the space. Obviously you cannot have a kitchen with 20 specific work areas if the total floor area of your existing kitchen is 5 × 7 feet, but you can and should plan for the most efficient and effective use of the existing space.

If you plan your kitchen according to functions, efficiency, your abilities with tools, financial resources and your available time, you should be able to create a kitchen that is attractive as well as useful. Once you have a complete work plan, the actual work is academic.

CHAPTER 3

COUNTER BASES

Almost anyone can build a base for a kitchen counter, kitchen island, or bathroom vanity, using a few simple hand tools, plywood, adhesive, nails, and a ruler. When you consider that a counter base is nothing more than a topless box (counter tops are covered in Chapter 4) you begin to see the simplicity of the project.

The basic material used for most commercially made counter bases (either kitchen or bathroom) is plywood or chipboard. It seems that the makers of the better counter bases use ¾-inch thick plywood, while the less expensive models are made with ⅝- or even ½-inch thick plywood or chipboard. My preference is to use ¾-inch thick plywood, finished on one side, unless the finished unit will be covered with plastic laminate. If the finished counter will be covered with paint or plastic laminate you can buy a grade of plywood which is less expensive than that which is finished on one side.

It may be helpful at this time to discuss some of the types of plywood that are available for building counter bases. The American Plywood Association recommends that you specify Medium Density Overlaid (MDO) plywood for excellent results when you plan to paint the finished counter. This grade of plywood has a smooth resin-treated fiber surface which is heat fused to the panel face and will take and hold paint beautifully. For most types of built-ins that will be painted, A-A, A-B, or A-D Interior type sanded plywood is recommended. Where a quality natural finish is required (waxed, sealed or varnished, for example) select fine grains panels in A-A, A-B, or A-D grades (Figure 3-1).

The best way to begin building a counter base is to know exactly the size you require, and to draw a scale diagram of the base. I usually draw several diagrams, one of the finished counter base, a rough sketch of the front, sides and a final diagram showing how all of the parts fit together. It is this last diagram—the one that appears exploded—that has all of the critical measurements indicated.

Without complicating things too much you should also show where drawers and doors are to be located. Remember that drawers will require some type of guidance system to slide on. Since drawers are covered in Chapter 7, I will only briefly mention that a provision should be made for them in the initial working diagram.

Height, depth and width are all important in the construction of a counter base. Remember, the height will be increased by the addition of a top, so you must know what type of top will be on the counter, as well as its thickness. Adjust the height of the counter base accordingly, which in all cases will be less the thickness of the counter top. Standard finished counter height, according to figures released by the U.S. Department of Agriculture (DOA), is a minimum of 30 inches and a maximum of 38 inches. A good working height for a finished kitchen counter is 37 inches, and this is the height of most of the kitchen counters I have built.

The depth of a kitchen counter, will in part be determined by the amount of available space you have in the kitchen. The same DOA report suggests that kitchen counters be a minimum of 24 inches and a maximum of 30 inches wide. Again, personal experience has proven that most kitchen counter depths are 28 inches. You may be influenced by existing fixtures in your kitchen—stove or refrigerator, for example—as to the depth of your kitchen counters. It is important to remember also that the top of the kitchen counter usually overhangs the counter base by at least 1 inch but usually not more than 3 inches.

Interior Type

Grade Designation (2)	Description and Most Common Uses	Typical Grade-trademarks	Veneer Grade — Face	Veneer Grade — Back	Veneer Grade — Inner Plies	Most Common Thicknesses (inch) (3)
N-N, N-A, N-B INT-APA	Cabinet quality. For natural finish furniture, cabinet doors, built-ins, etc. Special order items.	N N G1 INT APA PS1.74 / N A G2 INT APA PS1.74	N	N,A, or B	C	3/4
N-D-INT-APA	For natural finish paneling. Special order item.	N D G3 INT APA PS1.74	N		D	1/4
A-A INT-APA	For applications with both sides on view. Built-ins, cabinets, furniture and partitions. Smooth face; suitable for painting.	A A G1 INT APA PS1.74	A	A	D	1/4, 3/8, 1/2, 5/8, 3/4
A-B INT-APA	Use where appearance of one side is less important but two solid surfaces are necessary.	A B G1 INT APA PS1.74	A	B	D	1/4, 3/8, 1/2, 5/8, 3/4
A-D INT-APA	Use where appearance of only one side is important. Paneling, built-ins, shelving, partitions, and flow racks.	A-D GROUP 1 INTERIOR PS1.74 000	A	D	D	1/4, 3/8, 1/2, 5/8, 3/4
B-B INT-APA	Utility panel with two solid sides. Permits circular plugs.	B B G1 INT APA PS1.74	B	B	D	1/4, 3/8, 1/2, 5/8, 3/4
B-D INT-APA	Utility panel with one solid side. Good for backing, sides of built-ins. Industry: shelving, slip sheets, separator boards and bins.	B-D GROUP 3 INTERIOR PS1.74 000	B	D	D	1/4, 3/8, 1/2, 5/8, 3/4
DECORATIVE PANELS–APA	Rough-sawn, brushed, grooved, or striated faces. For paneling, interior accent walls, built-ins, counter facing, displays, and exhibits.	DECORATIVE BD G1 INT APA PS1.74	C or btr.	D		5/16, 3/8, 1/2, 5/8
PLYRON INT-APA	Hardboard face on both sides. For counter tops, shelving, cabinet doors, flooring. Faces tempered, untempered, smooth, or screened.	PLYRON INT APA			C & D	1/2, 5/8, 3/4

Figure 3-1: Plywood types for cabinets and built-ins.

The width of the kitchen counter base is usually the easiest of all the measurements to determine. Often there are limiting factors such as stove and refrigerator location, length of the room where the counter will be installed and location of the counter in the kitchen. Keep in mind that if you are planning to have an L shaped counter, there will be additional measurements to consider.

As mentioned earlier, it will be easier to construct a custom kitchen counter base if you think of the finished counter as a box or rectangle, and make modifications to this. Figure 3-2 illustrates the basic design of a kitchen counter base. You will note that the ends of the counter base are identical, but keep in mind that if either end will be exposed, the sanded side of the plywood must face outward (unless, of course, the entire counter will be covered with veneer or plastic laminate).

Also note that there is a toe or kick space at the front bottom of the counter base. This is standard in kitchen counter building and enables a person to stand at the counter without marring its face.

The front of the counter can have any combination of drawers, doors, or vents, providing, of course, that there is both balance and harmony in the finished counter.

As a side note I must mention that the doors which I make for counter bases are not flush, but are instead cut larger than the door opening and hung on the surface of the counter base. This type of door is commonly referred to as lipped or overlapped.

If you are building a counter base, for a bathroom for example, you will usually only have one door, and one internal shelf. A

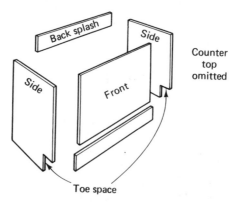

Figure 3-2:   The basic kitchen counter base design can also be used for bathroom vanities.

drawer is usually not included because the plumbing fixtures beneath the sink basin would obstruct its operation.

Since a bathroom vanity is really a small version of a kitchen counter base, I think it might be helpful to illustrate how to build this type of counter base, and later in this chapter show how this basic counter can be expanded to fill the needs of counters in the kitchen.

BUILDING A BATHROOM VANITY

The bathroom vanity described here is intended to have three exposed sides and the back fastened to an existing wall. Figure 3-3 illustrates how the finished bathroom vanity will look, as well as a side view. The dimensions listed are for a bathroom vanity of standard height, depth and width, and the materials list is for all parts necessary except sink and related plumbing parts (including back splash).

You will need the following parts to construct this bathroom vanity:

A • 2—20 × 33-inch ¾-inch plywood (sides)

B • 1—30 × 35-inch ¾ plywood (front)

C • 1—15 × 15-inch ¾-inch plywood (door)

D • 1—18½ × 33½ inch ¾-inch plywood (inside floor)

E • 1—20¼ × 35-inch ¾-inch plywood (top)

F • 1—1 × 3 × 35-inch kick plate

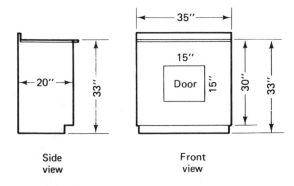

Figure 3-3:   The basic bathroom vanity design.

G • 1—1 × 8 × 35-inch back brace & back splash

H • 2—1 × 3 × 17-inch internal braces

I • 1—1 × 8 × 33½-inch back internal brace

J • 1—1 × 3 × 33½-inch backlip floor (attach to back base)

K • 2—1 × 1 × 15-inch top guides

L • 1 × 1 × 30-inch front top guide

   • 1—pound #8 finishing nails

   • 12—1½-inch wood screws

   • 2—hinges and a knob or handle

   • white glue

Begin by cutting out all of the necessary parts from two sheets of ¾-inch plywood, sanded on one side. Accuracy cannot be overstressed here because if the parts are not the exact measurements given, the finished vanity will not fit together as it should.

When the two side pieces (A.—2—20 × 33-inch) have been cut, it will be necessary to remove a 3 × 3-inch square from one of the corners. It may be best if you remove this section (which will allow for a kick plate) from the end of the sheet that has the factory edge. This edge, we must assume, is square and true and will ultimately come to rest on the floor of the bathroom. You will find that removing a 3 × 3-inch section will be easier to accomplish if you use either a hand saw or an electric sabre saw. Careful measuring, again, is the key to predictable results.

The next cut that must be made to both sides of the vanity is for the back splash, which will be located on the top back of the counter. Remove a section ¾-inch wide by 4-inches deep from the corner diagonally across from the corner where the toe space plate cut was made, as illustrated in Figure 3-4.

After these cuts have been made you can begin assembling the bathroom vanity. Start by attaching a 1 ×.3 × 17-inch piece to the bottom of each of the sides (Part H). Then attach a 1 × 1 × 15 inch piece to the top of each of the sides, Part K, and the same size stock to the top of the front (inside), also Part K.

To give you a better understanding of what is being done here: the 1 × 3 × 17 inch piece (Part H) along the bottom will ultimately become the resting place for the bottom of the vanity, and the top pieces (all 1 × 1 inch stock; Part K) are used for fastening down the top.

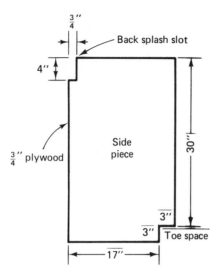

Figure 3-4: Make a cut for the back splash diagonally across from the cut made for the toe space.

I have found the best way to attach internal parts of this type into counters and vanities is to mark the position of the piece (¾ inch away from the ends of the piece), apply a bead of white glue to one side of the piece and reposition it on the side (or other large part of the counter) then screw it into place. Some carpenters simply nail these internal braces into place, while companies that make counters in stock sizes most commonly staple the pieces together. The glue and screw method is the most dependable though certainly not as quick as nailing or stapling (see Figure 3-5).

The next step is to attach Part J (1 × 3 × 33½ inch) to the bottom edge of Part I (1 × 8 × 33½ inch). This particular part will be the bottom back of the counter, and the floor of the counter will rest on the 1 × 3. These two parts are joined with glue and screws, in the same manner as the internal bracing above (see Figure 3-5). After these last two parts have been fastened together, the actual assembly of the counter can begin.

The counter will be easier to put together if you have someone help you with the initial assembly. Begin by attaching the bottom back plate (Parts I and J) to the bottom (inside, back) of the sides. This piece of 1 × 8 stock (with attached 1 × 3 stock) is attached by nailing through the bottom side of the vanity. Nail one side at a time. After the back bottom brace has been securely

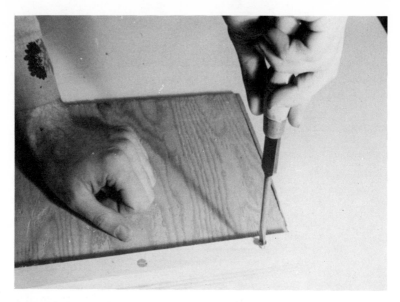

Figure 3-5:   For strength, glue and screw internal supports to the sides and front of vanity.

fastened to the side pieces, attach the front bottom brace (Part F) to the front of the counter. Note that this piece is face nailed to the area that will be the back of the kick plate or toe space (Figure 3-6).

Now, to add greater strength to the counter, attach the floor of the counter (Part D). If you have attached all of the internal bracing properly, and have made all of your cuts straight and true, the floor should fit right into place. You may want to first run a bead of white glue on top of all of the bottom bracing. Then nail the floor into place and countersink the heads with a nail set and hammer (Figure 3-7).

At this point in the construction, you can tip the vanity onto its back and attach the front. Care must be exercised so that the edges of the front piece align with the top, side and bottom edges of the vanity. Run a bead of white glue over the area that will come in contact with the front of the vanity, then nail the front piece into place.

Next, tip the vanity so that it is lying on its front and attach the back splash (Part G) to the top back of the counter. The counter should start becoming more rigid as you attach these parts, not to mention heavier as well.

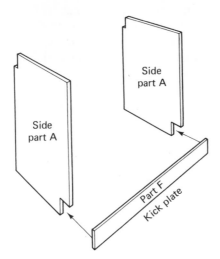

Figure 3-6:   The kick plate is face nailed to the front bottom of the vanity.

The last part to be attached is the top (Part E) of the vanity, and if everything has been done according to plan the top should lie right into place. This design calls for the top to be butted against the back splash, flush with the sides, and overhanging the front of the counter by 1 inch. The top is nailed into place after a

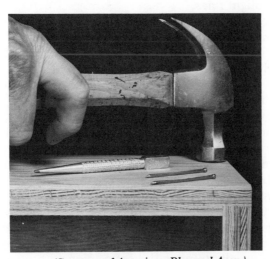

(Courtesy of American Plywood Assn.)

Figure 3-7:   Use a nail set and hammer to countersink nail heads.

bead of white glue has been applied first to the top edges of the vanity. If you should find that the top does not align quite perfectly with the sides and back of the vanity, you can work it into place by applying slight pressure to one of the front corners. This is best accomplished if the vanity is first placed with its back up against a solid surface such as a wall. Care must be exercised here for if you force the sides too much the finished vanity will not sit flat on the floor.

At this stage of the construction you should have a bathroom vanity with a solid front, that is, the hole for the door has not been cut out, but the vanity should stand firm by itself. To install the front door, begin by marking the location of the hole. In this case the opening will be 14 × 14 inches and will be centered on the front of the vanity. Lines are drawn 10½ inches in from each side and 8 inches down from the top and bottom of the vanity. After this hole or opening has been clearly marked you can cut out the section. This can be done in several ways, two of which I will discuss

Cut Outs

The first, and probably the easiest method is to use an electric sabre saw. First drill a hole large enough to accommodate the blade of the sabre saw. Then insert the saw blade, turn on the saw and cut out the opening. Work carefully so that the resultant opening has straight lines.

The other method of cutting out the opening is to make a plunge cut using an electric circular saw. (*Caution:* the plunge cut is dangerous and should only be attempted with both hands on the saw.) Begin making a plunge cut by resting the front edge of the saw on the face of the vanity (the vanity should be lying on its back with the front or face lying horizontal). The blade of the saw is over the mark and off the surface of the front. With both hands on the saw, press the trigger of the saw to start the motor, and after the saw has developed optimum speed, slowly lower the blade down to and through the surface. The blade should pass through the front of the vanity along the cutout line. Once the blade has passed through the face of the vanity, ease the saw forward until you are just about at the end of the line. Repeat this procedure for all four cutout lines. Work carefully and give this operation your fullest attention. After all of the cuts have been made you can usually tap out the cut section with a sharp rap from a hammer or your hand. If the section will not fall out easily, you may have to finish the corners with a hand saw (Figure 3-8).

Figure 3-8:   A plunge cut requires your full attention, as well as a firm, two-handed grip on the saw.

After the opening has been made check over the cut lines. Each should be straight and free of roughness. If any splinters or unevenness is present go over that area with a file or wood rasp. Work from the outside towards the inside of the vanity. When you are satisfied with the opening, you can install the door which will overlap the opening by 1 inch all around. (Hinge installation is covered fully in Chapter 8.)

After the door has been attached, you will want to make a cutout for the sink that is to be installed into the top of the bathroom vanity. A diagram or template is commonly supplied with new sinks and you simply lay this over the top, mark the area to be cut out and make the cut with an electric sabre saw. A sabre saw must be used as the hole will more than likely be round or oval. Before actually installing the sink, however, you should finish the vanity. In some cases this will amount to adding plastic laminate to the top (or tile) and painting, staining or applying a clear finish to the rest of the vanity. The inside of the vanity is usually painted white for ease of cleaning and visibility. (Laminates are covered in Chapter 4 and finishing is covered in detail in Chapter 9. Please refer to these chapters).

When the bathroom vanity has been finished to your satisfaction you can install it in your bathroom. Installation of vanities is simple and is covered in Chapter 10.

The bathroom vanity described above is simple to build and can be assembled in a few hours. The cost is easily half what you would pay for a prefinished model, the type sold in most home improvement centers across the country. Another favorable aspect of this vanity is that it is stronger and made to last longer than most of the prefinished types available. The materials used and the way this vanity is put together all add up to a unit that is made to endure and provide a lifetime of useful service.

If you would like to spend more time cutting and measuring, instead of simple butt joints you can make lap or beveled joints on this vanity.

Building a kitchen counter, while a project of greater magnitude, is basically the same as building a bathroom vanity. There are, however, a few points worth mentioning. In the first place a kitchen counter is usually longer than 35 inches. The internal structure of a kitchen counter is also different, having internal shelves, drawers (that slide), a venting system to help remove moisture and possibly other custom features, but the basic design remains the same. One other difference between a bathroom vanity and a kitchen counter is that the latter is usually built into place in the kitchen, mainly because of size, while a bathroom vanity can usually be built in the workshop and later installed in the bathroom.

BUILDING KITCHEN COUNTERS

Since the size of the kitchen counter you are building will be, in part, determined by the general layout and size of the kitchen, it is not possible to give more than general directions for building. However, all of the basic layout, construction, and finishing techniques are adaptable for any size kitchen counter.

The emphasis will be on how to make modifications and built-ins to the general design of a kitchen counter. Specifically, we will discuss internal shelving, doors (both sliding and hinged) internal bracing, vents, backs, and general assembly. (Drawers are discussed in detail in Chapter 7.)

Remember that the basic design of a kitchen counter is very similar to the bathroom vanity discussed earlier in this chapter. A kitchen counter will have a kick plate or toe space, it will have a floor, sides, front and top. Where a kitchen counter differs from a bathroom vanity is in the internal structure.

Generally speaking, a kitchen counter should have vertical supports every 24 inches (except for the area directly under a sink—this can be somewhat greater—up to 3 feet). Besides providing strength to a kitchen counter, internal supports are also necessary for the addition of internal shelves.

Internal Shelves

Basically there are three ways which you can build internal shelves into your kitchen counter; cleats, shelf supports or the shelves may be set into dado cuts.

The simplest way to install internal shelving in kitchen counters is to attach 1 × 2 inch stock to the internal walls of the unit. Then the shelves are simply laid on top of the shelf supports for a functional shelf. This system, while quite easy to install, does not allow for any variation of shelf height once the shelf supports have been installed. But, in many cases, the shelf height is predetermined and remains that way for the life of the unit (see Figure 3-9).

The second way to install internal shelves is to first attach either shelf brackets (see Figure 3–10) or to drill holes 2 inches

Figure 3-9:   The simplest way to install shelves is to first attach 1 × 2 inch shelf supports to internal walls of the counter base.

Figure 3-10: Internal shelf brackets can be installed inside the counter. These can be adjusted simply by repositioning the supports.

apart (vertically) and 1 inch in from the inside edge of the counter. Into these holes go metal shelf rests. With either of these shelf supports, the height of the shelf is variable. The shelf brackets are, of course, the easier of the two systems to install. The shelf brackets are attached to internal walls of the counter—two strips on each wall, then shelf rests are inserted in the shelf bracket at the required height. The shelf can then be set on the four supports.

Another way to install internal shelves in a kitchen counter involves dadoing shelf slots in the counter walls. This method makes shelf installation very easy, as the shelves simply slide into the dado slot. The dadoes, however, must be very carefully laid out and cut. Of course, dado cuts must be made to the counter's internal walls before the counter is assembled, so planning is crucial here. Setting up dado cuts is a bit easier with a template to guide with the cuts. I use a piece of scrap lumber with marks to indicate where the dado cuts are to be made. This dado cut indicator is similar to a story pole used in other forms of house construction—namely, house framing, and is commonly referred to as a layout rod.

Dado cuts are best made on a table saw or with a hand-held router. Old-time craftsmen used a chisel and a mallet for dado

(Courtesy of American Plywood Assn.)

Figure 3-11:   Dado cut slots for shelf supports are neat and strong, but care must be exercised when laying out the work.

cuts, but mastery of these tools takes many years of practice. You can master dado cuts with electric tools very quickly providing you lay out the work carefully (see Figure 3-11).

There are basically two types of doors that I install to either kitchen counters or bathroom vanities: hinged and sliding. As previously mentioned, all of the doors I install (other than sliding) are oversized—at least one inch larger on all measurements. These doors use semi-concealed hinges, are easy to hang, and have a neat, finished appearance. The material I use to make hinged doors is the same material I use to construct the rest of the counter—¾-inch thick plywood. In many cases I use plywood that has been sanded on both sides for doors unless the door will be finished with plastic laminate, in which case, a lesser grade plywood can be used. Chapter 8 on "Hardware" has a complete discussion of the other types of hinges used for hanging doors, including concealed pin hinges, and surface hinges. Please refer to this chapter when considering the types of hinges available. Keep in mind that semiconcealed hinges are the easiest to install and the finished appearance is not objectionable to most people.

Counter Doors

Sliding doors for kitchen counters, cabinets and bathroom vanities are common in American homes and are not difficult to make. The most common material for the construction of these doors is plywood (as in the construction of the rest of the counter), or plastic, glass and chipboard. These sliding doors slide in grooves cut into the cabinet frame or in tracks mounted on the edge of the counter frame. The tracks that the doors slide in can be made by making a plow cut (actually two) in from the front edges of both the top and bottom of the counter. Another method of creating tracks is to install strips of quarter round molding along the top and bottom edges of the counter; here square strips are used for the middle of the track. Generally speaking, the upper tracks are deeper than the lower tracks to enable you to take the doors out if the need should arise. Here, the doors are installed by pushing them upwards to the top track, enabling them to enter into the upper grooves first. Then, the doors are lowered so that the bottom edges drop into the lower tracks. Keep in mind that the larger the doors, the more resistance to sliding. For doors larger than two feet high, it is recommended that you use some type of metal sliding track and rollers, as these will compensate for the weight of the doors.

For a tighter fit in the tracks, you may want to make rabbet cuts along both the top and bottom edgees of the doors. Rabbet the back of the front door, and the front of the back door. This lets the doors almost touch, leaving just a small gap between the doors. This decreases the chances of dirt or dust entering and increases the overall depth of the counter. Generally speaking, the doors should be rabbeted half their thickness (see Figures 3-12 and 3-13).

Vents

The area around the kitchen or bathroom sink is prone to moisture problems and this should be given some consideration when building these types of counters. The best way to build in protection is to have some form of vent system that will enable moisture to escape. In older kitchen counters it was common to simply make horizontal cuts (at least 2 feet in length) to the face

Figure 3-12: For removable doors, plow the bottom grooves 3/16-inch deep. After finishing, insert door by pushing up into excess space in top groove, then dropping into bottom.

Figure 3-13: Close fitting plywood doors are made by rabbeting top and bottom edges of both doors. This lets doors almost touch, leaving little space for dust to get into the cabinet.

41

of the counter directly below the sink. In modern construction these vent cuts are considered unsightly and are rarely made. It is common practice now to add some type of face plate that has been blocked ½ to ⅝ of an inch off the surface of the counter face. This space will effectively provide the required venting for a kitchen sink. Another way to provide suitable venting is to make concealed vent cuts in the toe space, along the bottom of the counter.

Counter Backs

Most of today's modern kitchen counters and bathroom vanities do not have a back. They are really only three-sided, the back being an existing wall. But for added insulation or for when the back of the counter is visible, as in a kitchen island, for example, a back can be constructed.

There are several ways of attaching a back to a counter, which depends on the type of material chosen for the back, the type of tools to be used and the intended purpose of the back (e.g., is the back for strength, or just to cover up framing or a wall in poor condition).

The simplest method of attaching a back to a counter is to nail a piece of plywood (¼- or ⅜-inch) flush to the back of the counter. Simply measure the back of the counter, cut a piece of plywood the proper size and then install it using nails and if needed, white glue.

The standard method of applying backs to counters calls for rabbeting the internal sides of the counter (see Figure 3-14). The back in the left of this figure has been rabbeted just deep enough to take the new plywood back. The back in the right of the photo has been set into rabbet cuts that are slightly deeper than the back is thick. This will enable the counter to be mounted to a wall that is not quite flush or that is irregular.

One other, very simple, method of installing a counter back is to first install quarter round molding around the inside back of the counter. Then the back is cut to fit inside and rests on this molding. The back in this case is both nailed and glued for strength (Figure 3-15).

Internal Bracing

Just about all of the counters and vanities I build are made from ¾-inch plywood. You will notice, if you visit a local store that sells ready-made counters, that commercial countermakers do not

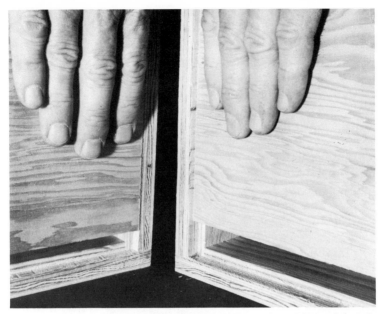

(Courtesy of American Plywood Assn.)

Figure 3-14: The standard method of applying a back to cabinets calls for rabbeting sides (inside) so back fits flush. An alternative is shown above on right. Rabbet cut is made ½-inch deeper so cabinet will fit flush against an uneven wall.

(Courtesy of American Plywood Assn.)

Figure 3-15: When only hand tools are used, attach strips of ¼-inch quarter-round molding for the back to rest against. Then glue and nail the back into place against the molding.

use plywood this thick. Instead, they use thinner plywood (or chipboard) and internal bracing. Although I do not recommend this cost cutting for the do-it-yourselfer, you can build counters and vanities less expensively using thinner plywood and internal bracing. Keep in mind, however, that while you will save on material costs, you will have a lot of extra work building the internal bracing.

Internal bracing must be installed wherever two sections of the counter intersect at a ninety degree angle (see Figure 3-16). Wherever this type of bracing is used, it should be installed using both nails and white glue for additional strength. In effect, what you are doing with internal bracing is building a frame which supports the lighter weight plywood.

Finishing and installing kitchen counters and bathroom vanities is covered in Chapters 9 and 10.

(Courtesy of American Plywood Assn.)

Figure 3-16:   Internal bracing should be used for strength, as in the right of photo, whenever plywood less than ¾-inch thick is used.

CHAPTER 4

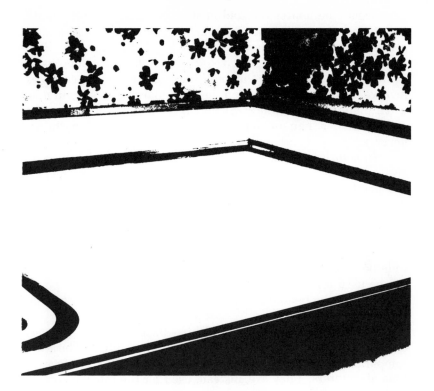

PLASTIC
LAMINATE TOPS

Tops for kitchen counters and bathroom vanities are very simple to build, being not much more than a piece of plywood that fits over the base unit. Modern counter tops are most commonly covered with plastic laminate for protection and beauty. Plastic laminates resist wear, burns, dirt, grease, and stains. They are easy to keep clean with liquid soap and water, and are the most practical choice for modern homes.

Plastic laminates (or Formica, which is actually one company's brand name), are sold with several different surface finishes such as gloss, satin, textured and brushed. Colors range from basic white to just about every color in the rainbow, and more. There are also natural wood grain patterns, as well as contemporary designs, a color, pattern and texture to suit everyone.

Plastic laminates are sold in sheet form, and in several different thicknesses. The most common for residential use is called general purpose or standard grade and it is 1/16-inch thick. Standard sheet widths are 24-, 30-, 36-, 48- and 60-inch, and lengths are 60, 72, 84, 96, 120, and 144 inches. Since plastic laminates are expensive, it is important to keep these standard sheet sizes in mind when planning the counter. If possible, build counter tops that will be smaller than any one of these combinations of widths and lengths.

In addition to the 1/16-inch thick standard grade, there are also special purpose grades of plastic laminate. These include: the postforming grade (about 1/20-inch thick), which can be heated and bent or formed around counter edges and backsplashes; and the vertical grade (about 1/32-inch thick), designed for vertical applications i.e., cabinet fronts, doors, and back splashes. You can usually find this grade cut into 1⅝- to 2-inch wide bands (commonly called edge trim or edge banding), which can be used for the edges of counter tops. Vertical grade plastic laminate can be heated and curved to conform to other than flat contours.

Another type of plastic laminate—backer sheets—are used on the underside of areas for dimensional stability. These are comparatively inexpensive but are not designed for the faces or tops of counters. They are, instead, used for the interiors of cabinets and as shelf covering.

In addition to being sold as sheets, plastic laminates are also available preattached to ¾-inch thick plywood or chipboard. These prefabricated plastic laminate sheets take a lot of the work out of building counter tops because all you have to do is attach a suitable back splash and finish off the edges of the sheet.

Still one other way to finish off a counter base is to buy a ready-made counter top. These are usually stocked in standard lengths and widths at most large lumber yards. Prefabricated plastic counter tops usually have a back splash and front lip molded in. Simply buy the right size top, bring it home and attach it to your counter base (and cut out the sink hole if a sink is to be included in the finished counter). Prefabricated counter tops are recommended for do-it-yourselfers who may not have the tools for properly laying and trimming plastic laminates, or for those who prefer to have special edges which require expensive equipment to make.

Many different types of adhesives can be used to attach plastic laminates to plywood counter tops but the best choice is contact cement. With this type of adhesive, bonding happens upon contact and, therefore, no clamping is necessary. Contact cement is applied with a small paint brush and allowed to dry before the two pieces are fitted together.

Counter tops are most often built from ¾ inch-thick plywood or chipboard. Generally speaking, it is better to choose a plywood with a waterproof glue for all counter tops, especially when the unit will be used in a high moisture area such as the bathroom or kitchen.

Figure 4-1 shows the basic design of a counter top and can be used for either kitchen counters or bathroom vanity tops. This particular top has a built-in back splash and an extended (overhanging) double thickness front edge. The purpose of the wide front edge is to make the overhang stronger and balance out the overall design of the counter. The side edges of this top are usually flush with the sides of the counter but can be extended over the sides for a different appearance (as well as added space), providing the counter does not have to fit between existing appliances or walls.

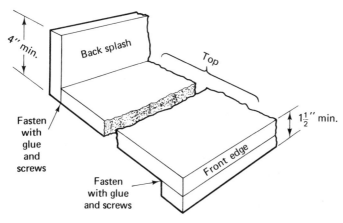

Figure 4-1: The basic counter top design can be used for either the kitchen or bathroom.

The top is first cut from a sheet of ¾-inch plywood to the proper dimensions for the counter. Then the back splash is attached with countersunk wood screws and white glue. Next, the front edge of the counter must be built up. This is most easily accomplished by adding an additional piece of ¾-inch thick plywood under and flush with the front edge. This additional piece is glued and screwed into place. Before the plastic laminate is attached, the counter top should be attached to the counter. (The top can be built and covered with plastic laminate in the workshop but it may be easier to work with the top in place.)

Because kitchen counter tops are usually long—at least 4 feet—it is important that the plywood sheet be cut as cleanly and straight as possible. If you are using a table saw, you should have little problem making the cut, but if you are using a hand-held circular saw, there is a lot of room for error unless you use some type of guidance system for the saw. The worst possible way to cut a sheet of plywood with a hand saw is the freehand method, commonly used in rough framing, where straight cuts are not crucial.

A simple guidance system for a hand saw can be quickly and easily set up using a few clamps and a straight-edge. The straight-edge can be a scrap piece of straight-edge lumber or a special metal straight-edge designed for marking. A straight 2 × 4, 8 feet long makes an ideal hand saw guide when securely fastened with clamps to a sheet of plywood (Figure 4-2).

Figure 4-2:   A simple but effective saw guide can be made with a few clamps and a straight piece of angle aluminum.

Another helpful hint for using a hand-held circular saw to cut ¾-inch thick plywood, is to use a carbide tipped blade in the saw. These blades rarely bind up, as do special plywood blades, and help you to cut straight, clean lines. You should also set the depth gauge of the saw so that the blade does not protrude more than ½ inch through the work. This will keep the saw blade cooler and make the saw easier to push through the work.

When marking the sheet of plywood for cutting, try to make the cuts so that one edge—the one that will face out from the counter—is the factory edge. The edge you cut will be the back of the counter. This way, if there is a slight variation or irregularity, it will be at the back of the counter and easier to conceal.

After the counter top has been cut, the back splash and front edge additions added, and the assembled counter top installed on the counter base, you should check the new top for squareness and flatness. Use a four foot level or other suitable instrument to check the top—it must be level. If it is not, ascertain what the problem is and correct it using shingle shims where necessary (see Figure 4-3). (Refer to Chapter 10, "Installation" for more details about installing counters.)

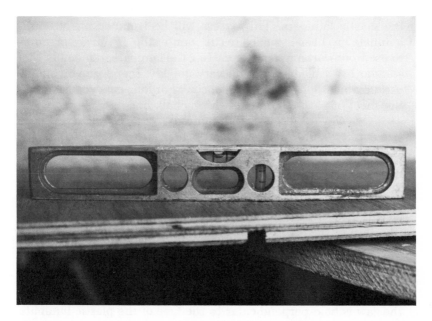

Figure 4-3:   Use a level to check that the counter top is flat and level.

Since plastic laminates are flat, the counter top must be checked before you can attach the laminate. The edges of the counter top are the areas to check thoroughly. Wherever two pieces are joined, check to see that the front edges are flat and square. A framing square is helpful for this type of checking. If there are front edge irregularities, correct them using a file for small areas and a saw for long edge irregularities. When you are satisfied that the entire counter top is flat, the edges square, and the top securely fastened to the base, you can begin attaching the plastic laminate.

Just about all plastic laminate work begins by attaching the laminate to the edges first, then the top. This way the horizontal surfaces will overlap the vertical surfaces and insure that there is less chance for moisture to seep down into the plywood.

CUTTING LAMINATES

There are several ways to cut plastic laminate and a few of them will be discussed. There are a few important things to keep in mind, however, no matter which method of cutting you choose. Since plastic laminates are hard, thin and brittle, always support the sheet on a solid surface when making cuts. Cut lines should be at least ½-inch wider and longer than the area to be covered with the plastic laminate. This excess will be trimmed off after the laminate has been attached to the counter top. If you are planning to use woodworking tools for cutting the laminate, remember that standard saw blades will dull very quickly, therefore you should use a carbide tipped blade for all cuts. For long cuts you can mark the sheet of plastic laminate with a chalk line.

One way to cut plastic laminates is to use a pointed tool such as a utility knife (changing the blade as necessary to keep it sharp), awl or an ice pick. Using one of these tools, the face of the plastic laminate is scored along the cut line until the sheet is almost in two. You will have to make several passes over the face before you reach this depth, so work carefully. After scoring the face of the sheet to about half its depth, the sheet is bent upward (the face of the sheet is up) and it should break along the score mark. This method is handy for irregular cuts, but is easily the most laborious of all cutting methods (see Figure 4-4).

You can also use a hand crosscut saw (12 points per inch) or a hacksaw (32 teeth per inch) providing the cut is not too long and the saw is held perpendicular to the face of the plastic laminate.

Electric power tools are the easiest way to cut plastic laminates. These include a table saw, hand-held circular saw, sabre

Figure 4-4:   Plastic laminate can be cut by scoring the face of the sheet with a sharp tool, then bending along the score line. The sheet should break along this line. Note that a straight piece of scrap lumber is being used as a straight edge.

saw and a portable router. If you are using a table saw, the sheet must be face up; this way any chipping of the laminate will be confined to the back, rather than the face of the work.

A hand-held circular saw can be used to cut laminates but the sheet should be securely fastened (face up) to a solid surface, and some type of guidance system should be used to guide the saw along the cut line. Remember that a carbide tip blade will not dull very much, while a standard blade will be almost useless after cutting a sheet of plastic laminate.

If you are using a sabre saw to cut plastic laminates, it is important to keep the face of the work down. This will insure that any chipping is on the back or underside of the material.

A portable router can be used to cut plastic laminates, and, in fact, this is the tool that enables you to obtain professional looking edges on the finished counter. Using a carbide tipped mica cutter, and a guidance system, you will be able to make exact cuts for edge material or other small areas that are tough to trim later on. It is important when using a router to cut plastic laminates to have the sheet material on a solid surface while making cuts.

As mentioned earlier, vertical surfaces are covered first with the laminates, then the horizontal surfaces. This means that the front, and possibly one or more sides of the counter and the face of the back splash are covered first. Measure these areas, and cut pieces of plastic laminate to slightly larger dimensions than required. Then check the pieces to make sure they are about right before applying the contact cement.

Contact cement is applied with a paint brush in an even coat (Figure 4-5). Two coats are applied to the face of the plywood and one to the back of the plastic laminate pieces. Then, the contact cement is allowed to dry a few minutes, depending on the temperature. Generally speaking, when the contact cement is dry to the touch it is ready to act as the bonding agent.

Figure 4-5:   Contact cement is easy to apply with a paint brush. Always read the label before use as some contact cements are extremely flammable, and others are toxic.

Before applying the contact cement, read the label to find out about manufacturer's cautions, and any special directions. Most contact cements are suitable for plastic laminate work but some are highly flammable and others are toxic. Ventilation should be provided and there should be no open flame in the area. Check the label for safety before use.

After the contact cement has dried, you can attach the vertical pieces to the counter. Remember, while working with contact cement, once contact has been made it will be difficult or impossible to reposition the plastic laminate. Once the two surfaces (which have been covered with contact cement) meet, bonding takes place. This fact cannot be overemphasized.

For small pieces, such as edges, you may find it helpful to start at one end and work across the face of the counter. Hold the edge strip close, but away from the counter edge. Place one edge of the plastic laminate along the edge of the counter, then slowly and carefully press the strip into place. Since the edge strip will be trimmed with the router, your only real concern is to make sure that the entire edge is covered with a piece of plastic laminate (Figure 4-6).

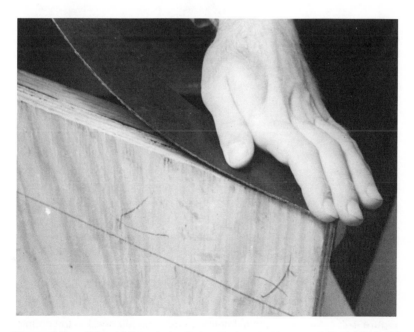

Figure 4-6:   Edge strips of plastic laminate must be carefully positioned before contact is made.

If the sides of the counter edge are to be covered with plastic laminate, they should be covered before the front face edge. This will hide the side edge joint of the laminate and result in a front edge that shows no edge joints.

After the edge strips have been pressed into place, and the contact cement is beginning to hold, you must go over the area and apply additional pressure to insure a complete and total bond. Professional plastic laminate installers use a roller to apply pressure to newly applied counter tops. You can also use a roller or a block of soft wood and a hammer. Make sure the block (2 × 4 × 8-inch piece of scrap lumber) is clean and smooth. You might want to attach a piece of rug or carpet to the block for additional protection (a carpet tile is very convenient to use for this). Pass the block over the work and strike it with the hammer to make sure solid contact has been made (Figure 4-7).

Figure 4-7:   After the plastic laminate has been attached to the counter top, use a roller or block and hammer to apply additional and heavy pressure over the entire surface.

TRIMMING PLASTIC LAMINATES

The next step is to trim off the excess plastic laminate using a portable router and special plastic laminate bit. This "Formica bit," as plastic laminate router bits are often referred to, is most often a carbide cutter with a pilot bearing at the bottom of the cutter (Figure 4-8). It is very simple to use and makes short work out of edge trimming. Simply place the router flat on the surface being trimmed (with the motor running but the bit not in contact with the plastic laminate). Then, slowly push the router into the work until contact is made. The Formica bit will cut through the excess plastic laminate and stop cutting as soon as the pilot bearing comes into contact with the flat surface (in this case the top or bottom of the counter top). Push the router along the edge and let the Formica bit do the cutting and trimming on the edge. Just before you come to the end of the counter, stop the motor and remove the router from the work. A router cutter works most efficiently when it is pushed into the work rather than pushed out; therefore, the ends of the counter edge should be trimmed separately. Simply push the router into the edges from the outside.

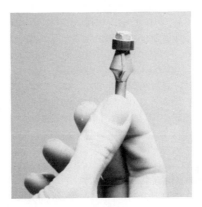

Figure 4-8:   The plastic laminate bit is used in a router for trimming the edges of counters.

Plastic laminate trimming with a router results in quite a bit of airborne chips. For safety, you should wear goggles or a protective face shield. This will enable you to closely watch what you are doing and prevent the possibility of eye damage.

After the edges have been covered with plastic laminate, and the excess material trimmed off with the router, you can attach the top piece of laminate to the counter. As with the edges, measure carefully, then cut a piece of plastic laminate to fit slightly larger than the area to be covered. Next, check the piece for fit. If you are satisfied with the fit, apply contact cement to the top of the counter and the back of the plastic laminate piece. When both surfaces are dry, press the plastic laminate into position on the counter top.

Since counter tops are usually large surfaces and contact cement can be difficult to work with since bonding takes place as soon as contact is made, you want to be certain that the laminate is positioned correctly before contact is made. There are two things you can do to prevent contact while positioning the laminate top onto the counter. Both involve placing something between the two surfaces to prevent bonding.

The first method is the dowel method. After the contact cement has dried to the touch, ½-inch diameter dowels are laid on top of the counter. The dowels must be longer than the counter is wide, so you can get them out later. Lay the plastic laminate on the dowels and position it so that the back edge butts up against the back splash area. When you are satisfied with the fit, slowly pull the dowels out and let the two surfaces meet. As you withdraw the dowels it is important to keep the plastic laminate in the desired position. Once the dowels have been removed to the point where contact has been made along the back edge, you are just about home free and can totally withdraw the dowels. The next step is to apply final pressure, with either a roller or block and hammer over the entire counter top surface.

The other method to prevent contact of the two surfaces while positioning the laminate on the counter top involves the use of two pieces of heavy brown paper. After you are satisfied with the fit of the plastic laminate to the counter top, apply the contact cement to both surfaces and let it dry. Then lay two sheets of heavy brown paper over the counter top. The papers must be wider and longer than the counter top, or obviously, bonding will take place as soon as the laminate and counter top make contact. The key here is that the contact cement will not adhere to a surface unless it also has a layer of contact cement. Position the plastic laminate on the counter top and, when you are satisfied with the joint along the back edge and sides, slowly remove one sheet of the brown paper. Then, ever so carefully, start to remove the second and final sheet of paper. Make sure that the back and side edges remain in position as you slip the paper from between the counter top and plastic laminate. Press on the laminate as you withdraw the paper to insure bonding. After the heavy brown paper has been totally removed, roll the surface or tap with a block and hammer to insure total bonding.

The next step is to trim off the excess plastic laminate around all the top edges of the counter. As described earlier, the trimming is most easily done with a hand-held router and a special plastic laminate trimmer. While working, keep an eye on the cutter blade in the router. If it should become covered with contact cement, as it surely will, stop the router, unplug for safety sake, and clean the cutter with either solvent or a sharp knife. The router bit will cut most efficiently if it is clean. Some professionals always spray the cutter with a silicone lubricant (such as WD-40) to prevent the buildup of contact cement and cut down on friction (Figure 4-9).

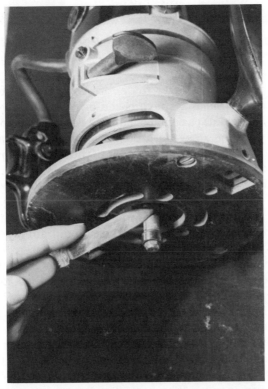

Figure 4-9:   Check your router bit often; a dirty bit does not cut well. If your router bit becomes clogged with contact cement, scrape it with a sharp knife.

After all the excess plastic laminate has been trimmed off with the router, you must go over all cut surfaces with a file, for a final smoothing. Work the file downward along the top of the counter at a 20 to 30 degree angle. This will bevel the edge slightly and give the counter a professional looking finished edge (Figure 4-10).

Figure 4-10:   Finish off the edges with a file, held at a 20 to 30 degree angle to the surface.

At this time, look over the entire counter and remove any contact cement that may have oozed out. Use a solvent recommended by the contact cement manufacturer, and a soft cloth.

Most counter tops—bathroom or kitchen—have a sink, and the time to cut out a sink hole is after the counter top has been attached to the base and covered with plastic laminate. There are a few different types of sinks—self rimming and metal rim, for example, but they are all installed in about the same way. The location of the sink is marked on the counter top, after first taking into consideration such things as water lines and drain pipes.

Most new sinks come packed with a template which is very helpful for marking the counter top prior to cutting out the sink hole. Generally speaking, the hole should be only slightly larger than the sink itself providing a metal rim is supplied with the sink. The decorative metal rim covers the space between the edge of the sink and the edge of the hole. Self-rimming sinks require a hole that is smaller than the outside edge of the sink. If you are uncertain about the sink hole or if the directions that came (or should have come) with the sink do not explain the hole size fully, ask about the opening. The best place to get information about the size hole for a sink is the lumber yard or plumbing supply store where you bought the sink.

To cut out a sink hole, the best tool is a hand-held electric sabre saw. First drill a hole large enough to accommodate the blade of the sabre saw, then cut out the opening, carefully following the markings on the counter top. After the hole has been cut, finish off the edges with a file, then install the sink. Before fastening down the sink you should first apply a bead of caulking around the edge of the sink (under the molding) to insure a waterproof joint.

If the counter top already has a sink hole cut before attaching the plastic laminate, you can make the sink hole cutout with the same router and plastic laminate bit used to trim the edges of the counter.

Although the joint where the top meets the back splash will be watertight, some professionals like to run a bead of caulking along this joint. Still other counter builders add a strip of chrome molding (quarter-round) to this joint after a bead of caulking has been applied. Personally, I feel this is not only unnecessary, but is a bad idea because the chrome along this area serves as a dirt catcher, and is tough to keep clean.

So far this chapter has discussed only one edge treatment for counter tops. In addition to the edge banding treatment, the front exposed edges of counter tops can be finished off in several other ways.

In older homes, chrome metal edging will often be found around the edges of kitchen counters (Figure 4-11). This extruded

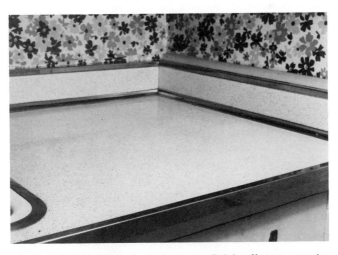

Figure 4-11:   Metal edging is one way to finish off your counter. Note the strip of chrome along the backsplash joint.

metal edge material is still available and is quite easy to install. It is two sided and L-shaped. The top of the counter is first covered with plastic laminate and after the edges have been trimmed, the chrome edge material is fastened to the edge. Either a waterproof adhesive, finishing nails or screws are used to attach the chrome edge. Probably the main reason that chrome edge material is not very widely used these days is that when installed there is a metal lip around the counter which can be an annoyance.

Another edge treatment involves the use of a wooden face strip along the edge. There are several variations of this edge treatment, some easy for the do-it-yourselfer and others hinging on absurd exercises in wood cutting and fitting.

The simplest alternative edge treatment uses a solid strip of hardwood—from ½- to 1-inch thick by 2- to 4-inches wide. The hardwood face strip can be glued, nailed or screwed to the edge face of the counter. The strip is attached after the plastic laminate top has been fastened to the counter top. It is important that the top edge of the hardwood strip is attached to the face of the counter so that the top edges are flat. Sometimes hardwood strips are a bit warped and you must make the fitting and then finish off with a small hand plane or spoke shave.

Another edge treatment uses three-quarter round molding attached to the front edge of the counter. This is simple to accomplish but this edge will take a lot of abuse, especially if the counter is in the kitchen, so a hardwood such as oak should be used.

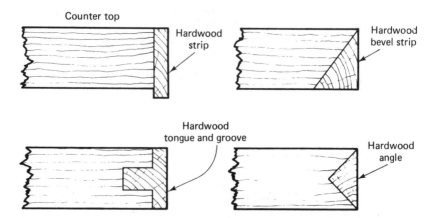

Figure 4-12:   Alternative edge treatments can add a distinctive look to your plastic laminate counter top.

Other edge treatments are shown in Figure 4-12 and, as you can see, they require some careful measuring and cutting. The tongue and groove edge is a nice exercise in the use of power tools as is the triangular insert. The bevel edge treatment can be done on a table saw.

Wooden edging on plastic laminate tops is distinctive and will add a special custom look to your counters. The wooden strips or moldings should, however, be protected with some type of coating. Probably the best choice is a few light coats of polyurethane, especially in the kitchen. This clear coating stands up well to wear and will keep your counter edge looking good for many years. For more information on polyurethane and other clear finishes (which let the natural beauty of the wood show through), see Chapter 9 on "Finishing."

Plastic laminated counter tops are found in just about every modern American home. They are very easy to keep clean, almost indestructible, and provide years of beautiful service. For other alternatives to counter top coverings you will have to read the next chapter which discusses tile and natural wood counter tops.

CHAPTER 5

TILE AND
OTHER TOPS

In addition to counter tops covered with plastic laminate, which were discussed in Chapter 4, there are several alternatives for the home craftsman. These include ceramic tile, and hardwood counter tops. Either of these two materials, when installed and finished correctly, will provide years of functional beauty, while at the same time serving to make your counter top a focal point in your kitchen.

Ceramic tile at one time was confined to the bathroom because it could provide a sanitary, moisture resistant surface. During the past ten years, however, ceramic tile has been receiving more attention from designers, homeowners and do-it-yourselfers. It has been coming out of the bathroom and finding its way into other areas of the home. Colors have changed quite a bit as well, no longer limited to only white. Now, almost every color in the rainbow is represented in ceramic tile. Additionally, textures are available, including brick, flashed bark, cobblestone, river-polished pebbles, tide-rippled sand, parquet, and even bamboo. Square sizes of modern ceramic tile range from one to twelve inches and shapes include rectangles, octagons, hexagons, Moorish curves and others.

Ceramic tile is also a good investment. It is resistant to wear, impervious to stains, withstands very high temperatures, and can be cleaned with a damp cloth. Ceramic tile is competitively priced when compared to plastic laminate counter tops of about the same dimensions.

Lastly, ceramic tile counter tops are very easy to install, as we will see later in this chapter. Special tools are needed only for special cutting and they can usually be rented for just a few dollars a day.

Solid wooden counter tops, while more expensive to construct and time consuming to make, provide a warm, custom look in the kitchen. Wooden tops can be made in the ever popular "butcher block" design, from wide planks or can be a collage of pieces, fitted together, then "frozen" or suspended in a bath of fiberglass cloth and resin.

Wooden counter tops are most commonly made from clear maple stock, but other hardwoods can be used for a darker or lighter overall look. Veneers are not recommended for wooden kitchen counter tops because cutting, chopping, and just plain traffic will tend to wear away the veneer layer within a few years. Solid pieces, on the other hand, will stand up well to use and, if the need should arise, can be sanded and refinished with little worry about damage to a thin top layer.

While you may not want—or cannot afford—to have a full wooden kitchen counter top, you might want to consider building and installing a section in your kitchen with this type of top. A 2 × 3 foot wooden counter section close to the sink, for example, where you can cut and prepare vegetables or meats, might add a distinctive touch as well as functionality. A cutting board type of counter insert makes a lot of sense as it can be removed and cleaned if necessary.

Since the construction of ceramic tile counter tops and wooden counter tops involves the use of different materials, tools and techniques, we will cover each type individually.

CERAMIC COUNTER TOPS

Ceramic tile is most commonly laid directly over a ¾-inch thick plywood counter top, similar to the counter tops discussed in the previous chapter. There are a few modifications, however, for strength and appearance which must be made to the basic counter top design.

Figure 5-1 shows the underside of a kitchen counter, with the addition of bracing for strength. Under counter bracing can be strips of ¾-inch plywood, 3-inches wide, and attached on edge. The length of these braces will be determined by the width of the counter base, as they are most effective when installed the entire width of the counter top but concealed by the front of the counter base. Braces are glued and screwed to the counter top from the top of the counter. The location of the braces is marked, then countersunk drill holes are bored through the top of the counter and finally, the braces are attached with screws and white glue. When the top is installed on the counter base, you should also fasten the ends of the braces through the front of the cabinet.

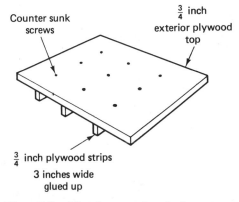

Figure 5-1: The underside of a counter, to be covered with ceramic tile, should have bracing attached. Strips of ¾-inch thick plywood, 3 inches wide can be attached on edge for effective bracing.

Ceramic tile counter tops do not usually have a back splash, per se, but instead usually have a tile covered wall behind the counter. This makes building a counter top base a bit easier because the 4-inch back splash is eliminated.

One variation of the standard 4-inch back splash (¾-inch thick) might be the addition of a back splash that has some width.

This can be a step type shelf at the back end of the counter. When planning this type of back splash take into consideration the size tile you will be using, and make the step one or two tiles high and one or two tiles wide. Build this type of back splash shelf with ¾-inch thick exterior plywood, then simply attach the tiles after the top has been installed on the counter base.

Other variations of the back splash shelf are easy to see; you could use a strip of hardwood for a face of the shelf and cover the top with tile or reverse this, having the tile on the face and a hardwood board for the shelf (see Figure 5-2).

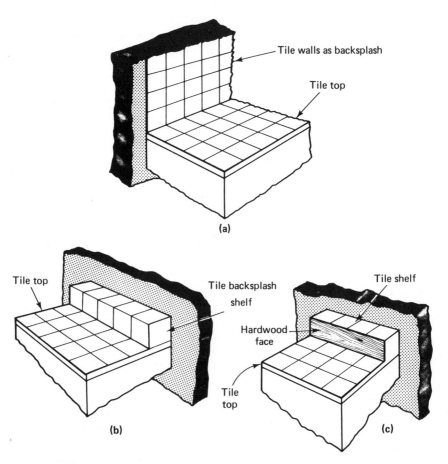

Figure 5-2:   Variations of the standard counter top backsplash include: (a) tile wall, (b) tile shelf, and (c) tile shelf with hardwood face or tile face and hardwood top.

Another area to consider is the front of the counter, where several different edge treatments are possible. Probably the simplest way to finish off the front edge of a tile covered kitchen counter is to attach a 4-inch wide (about 1-inch thick) piece of hardwood. The hardwood board's top edge should be flush with the top of the tile on the counter top, so you may want to install the board after the tiles have been set.

If you would like to keep your tile kitchen counter all tile, you can attach a tile front. To do this you must first attach a piece of ¾-inch plywood to the front of the counter. Needless to say, a bit of planning is involved here, as you want the tile joints to be equally spaced even though you are, in effect, coming over the edge with tile. Several tile manufacturers offer a trim or edge tile (see Figure 5-3) that tends to make face tile installation easier.

Details at sink

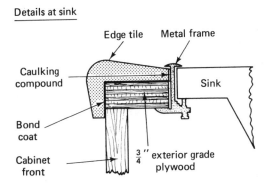

Section through countertop

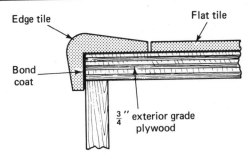

Figure 5-3: Several tile manufacturers offer special edge tiles. These tiles make it easy to cover the edge of a counter with tile.

While still planning the kitchen counter top, you must decide what shape, size or combination of tiles you will be using. Pay a visit to your local building supply or home improvement center to look over the selection. The choices include mosaic tile, commonly 1 by 1 inch square tiles which are sold in sheets; square tiles—2, 4, 6, 8, 10 and 12 inches on a side; octagonal; hexagonal; and other shapes. When planning, take into consideration the dimensions of your counter top, as well as how you will treat the edges and back of the counter. Purchase a size and shape tile that will be easy to work with.

Laying Ceramic Tile on Counter Tops

Before you can begin to set ceramic tile on a counter top you must first install a ¾-inch thick piece of exterior grade plywood to the counter base. The top should be level and securely fastened to the base cabinet. Then, if a sink is to be installed in the finished counter, you must determine its location and cut out a suitable hole. The next step is to sand and clean the surface of the counter top. Ceramic tile will be set into a bed of adhesive so the surface must be clean, dry and level enough to let the adhesive do its job.

After the surface has been sufficiently prepared, you can begin marking layout lines on the counter top. Ideally, the counter top should be a size that will hold an even number of uncut tile. Unfortunately, however, a row of tiles must sometimes be cut, and the layout lines will help you to determine this. If a row of tile must be cut, make it the back row, along the back splash area. The layout lines also help keep the rows of tile straight, as the first course of tile is set along these lines.

If you are covering a small counter top with ceramic tiles, you can do away with the layout lines and simply lay dry tiles on the counter top to see if any need to be cut.

In any event, once you have determined if tiles have to be cut or not, you can apply a coat of adhesive to the plywood counter top.

The adhesive you will use to set the tiles on the counter top should be the type recommended by the tile manufacturer. There are several types of tile adhesive—waterproof and semiwaterproof, for example—so make sure you have the right type.

The adhesive is spread on the counter top with a notched trowel in a smooth layer. The depth of the adhesive will be determined by the depth of the notches in the trowel you are using. Directions on the label should tell you the size trowel to use, but if they don't, ask where you purchased the tile. If the counter top is small, you can apply the adhesive to the entire surface, but if the counter is long or large, spread only a small area at a time—2 × 3 foot, for example.

Before the adhesive dries, you should begin installing the tile. Each tile should be set into the adhesive with a slight twisting motion, to insure solid and firm contact. As you set the first row of tiles into the adhesive, you should make certain that they are being laid according to the guideline or some other aid to alignment.

Most ceramic tiles have spacer nubs around the edges of the tile and, therefore, the spaces between the tile should almost automatically be even and uniform. Continue laying the tiles into the adhesive until the entire counter is covered. Lay in straight lines, and complete one row before beginning another, this will insure alignment. Do not, however, slide the tiles into position, as this tends to cause a build up of adhesive around the edges of the tiles (Figure 5-4).

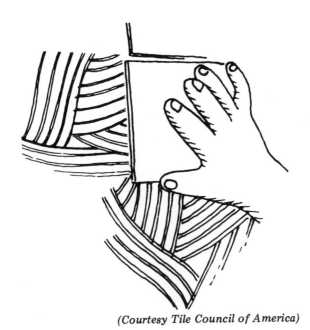

(Courtesy Tile Council of America)

Figure 5-4:   Set each tile with a slight twisting motion. Press firmly into place. Align tile so all points are uniform and straight.

If a row of tiles has to be cut, a tile cutter will save you a lot of time and help you to cut the tiles straight. A tile cutting machine can usually be rented for a few dollars a day from the store that sold you the tile. It is a simple machine to use. Simply mark the face of the tile, score this line with the cutter and the tile should break along the cut line. The cut edge should then be smoothed with a carborundum stone to remove any rough or sharp edges. Set the cut tile as you would any other.

It is a good idea not to cut more than one tile at a time, as the tile on one end of a row is liable to be larger or smaller than the tile on the other end of a row. Cut as you go along for the best fit.

If you have to fit tile around an irregular opening, such as a sink hole, you will find that a pair of tile nippers will help cut the tile easily. Tile nippers are very much like a pair of pliers except that the tips are usually carbide. Tile nippers are very easy to use. As the name implies, nip off bits of the tile until the desired shape is made. The key to using tile nippers is to remove small pieces at a time, for if you try to take off too much, the tile will most likely break (Figure 5-5).

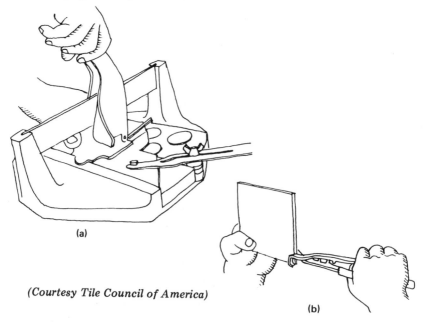

(a)

(Courtesy Tile Council of America)

(b)

Figure 5-5:   A tile cutter (a) can be rented from the store that sold you the tile. Ask for instructions for use. Tile nippers (b) are similar to a pair of pliers and are simple to use.

After all of the tiles have been set into the adhesive on the counter top, you should place a flat board on top of the tiles and tap with a hammer. This action will insure that a solid bond has been achieved and will also serve to flatten the surface. Slide the board over the surface as you tap with the hammer. Make sure that no tile edge is higher than another. You may want to use a level to check the finished job.

The next step is to wait 24 hours for the adhesive to set, then apply grout to all of the spaces between the tiles.

Grout is available as a dry powder which must be mixed with water before use, and premixed. I prefer the premixed grout for simplicity's sake. Make sure you purchase a waterproof grout for your counter top. The standard color for grout is white, but colors are available as well. Consider creating a different effect by using a grout that will contrast and accent the tile.

All grout is applied in the same manner. Spread the grout over the surface of the tiles, forcing the grout down into the spaces between the tiles. You may find a piece of dowel or the handle of a toothbrush handy for forcing the grout between the tiles (see Figure 5-6). You may also find a rubber float or squeegee handy for spreading the grout over the tiles. The point is to get as much grout into the spaces between the tiles as possible.

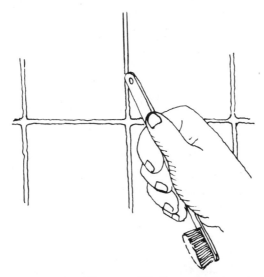

(Courtesy Tile Council of America)

Figure 5-6: To shape the grout lines on a tiled counter top, strike the joints with the handle of a toothbrush or rounded edged wooden dowel.

When you are satisfied that you have forced grout into every tile joint, remove the excess grout with a rubber squeegee (Figure 5-7). Then let the grout set until it becomes firm. The last step after the grout has hardened is to clean the face of the tile with a damp sponge. Once cleaned thoroughly, the surface should be buffed with a soft, dry rag.

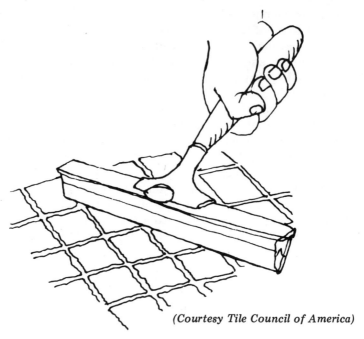

(Courtesy Tile Council of America)

Figure 5-7:   Remove the excess grout with a rubber squeegee after you have forced grout into all the tile joints.

A tile counter top correctly installed should provide many years of durable service and beauty. If ever the grout between the tiles should become loose or crumbly, you should remove the rotten grout, clean the joint, then reapply grout to the affected area. Other than occasional polishing, your ceramic tile counter top should last a lifetime (Figure 5-8).

SOLID WOODEN COUNTER TOPS

The most expensive kitchen counter tops to build are those which are made from solid pieces of hardwood; these can also be the most attractive. The hardwoods most suitable for kitchen

(Courtesy Tile Council of America)

Figure 5-8:   A ceramic tile counter properly installed should provide a lifetime of beautiful service.

counter tops include maple, oak, cherry, walnut, butternut, basswood, ash, birch, elm, hickory and beech, all deciduous trees. For an unusual effect, you can use several types of hardwood strips, placed so the different colors and tones enhance the total look of the counter top.

Working with solid hardwood is different from working with softwoods or laminated panels (plywood), but you can make the work a bit easier by purchasing the right type of hardwood and having some of the necessary operations performed at the lumber yard or mill.

Probably the best and easiest type of hardwood kitchen counter top to build is one which uses 2 × 2 inch thick pieces of hard maple. When you purchase the maple, make sure that it is seasoned i.e., most of the moisture has been removed, and therefore the lumber will not shrink or warp with time; and clear. Ask for first or seconds or 1 and 2 clear, as these are the highest quality, being almost free of blemishes. Another requirement of the hardwood you will be using is that it be straight and surfaced on all four sides (S4S). S4S means that the board has been planed on all four sides and each side is flat, smooth, and square. If you buy lumber with these designations—seasoned, clear, S4S—you will avoid many potential problem areas. You will also be buying the most expensive type of hardwood, but you will have an attractive investment.

If you are fortunate enough to own a table saw, or radial arm saw, and a jointer/planer, you will be able to purchase hardwood lumber that is rough cut—2 × 6, 2 × 8 or 2 × 10 inch dimensional lumber for example. Then, using your own power tools, perform some of the functions that tend to jack up the price of seasoned hardwood. If you do not own stationery power tools, or are not willing to cut and plane the boards yourself, you would be better off to pay a few dollars more and have these tasks done at the mill or lumber yard. This will save time and you can be certain that the work has been done correctly, but it will cost extra.

We will discuss how to build a butcher block type kitchen counter top. This type of top utilizes 2 × 2 inch maple with all of the requirements listed above—clear, seasoned and S4S. Using your imagination, and some of the tasks discussed in other parts of this book you will have no problem making modifications to this basic design.

Gluing

The simplest and quickest way to build a butcher block type counter top is to cut the strips of 2 × 2 inch thick maple stock to the required length, and then glue the strips together. You could use doweled joints, tongue and grooved joints or groove and spline joints if you want, but the excess work is not really necessary. The glue will hold the top together, providing the right type of glue is used and it is applied correctly.

There are several different types of adhesives that are suitable for constructing wooden counter tops—solvent type glues, water type glues and hide glue. It is important to choose the right type of glue for building a wooden counter top or you may find yourself regluing the counter at some point in the future. Each of these types of glues has certain properties which make them suitable for use (Figure 5-9).

Figure 5-9: Choose the right type of adhesive for gluing your wooden counter top together.

Solvent type glues consist of an adhesive base (vinyl resin or acrylic resin) and a solvent which makes the glue spreadable. As the solvent evaporates, the adhesive sets. Usually solvent type glues will have a reference to one or more of the following ingredients on the label: toluene, methyl ethyl ketone and acetone. Of the two types of resin, the acrylic is probably stronger than the vinyl. Contact cement is a solvent type glue but beware of the cautions on the label—some are highly flammable and others are toxic.

Water type glues are similar to solvent type glues except they take longer to set up. However, water type glues are lass expensive to buy and, of no small consequence, they are safe to use, being neither flammable or toxic. Probably the most familiar example of a water type glue is Elmer's Glue-All. A better choice for gluing strips of hardwood together is Elmer's Professional Carpenter's Wood Glue.

Hide glue, or animal glue as it is often called, is actually made from the hooves, bones and hides of animals. Hide glue is one of the oldest forms of glue, and there are several ways in which it is sold: powder, liquid, and flake. The most practical form of hide glue for the do-it-yourselfer is the liquid form, which can be used straight from the bottle providing the temperature is not under 70 degrees Farenheit. It is an excellent glue for joining woods, but clamping is necessary. Another point in hide glue's favor is that it is one of the best gap filling adhesives available. If joints are not exaxctly perfect the hide glue will take up the difference.

Before you begin applying the glue (whichever type) to opposite edges of the maple stock, you should first arrange the pieces so that the grains are alternated, as in Figure 5-10. This will help prevent cupping. You should also have the grain of each piece running in the same direction as all of the other pieces. One other point about grain and coloration as well, is that you should try to arrange the pieces so the overall look of the counter top is interesting. Hardwood is beautiful, so work with this beauty.

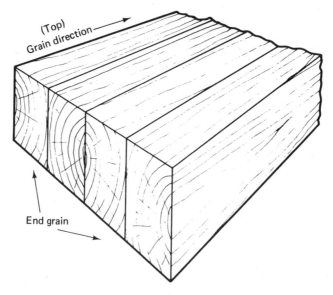

Figure 5-10 Alternate the grain of the hardwood strips to avoid cupping.

Apply the glue, either as it comes from the squeeze bottle or with a brush, to both sides of the maple stock. Do not apply too much glue or it will ooze out excessively when the boards are clamped together. If you are using a squeeze bottle, as you run the line of glue, beads should appear. When the glue is being applied at about the right rate, these beads will be about two inches apart. If you are spreading the glue with a brush, which is the best way, spread the glue evenly and thinly.

As you glue each piece, lay it on a work table in approximately the position it will be in for clamping. Each additional piece (with glue applied) should be butted up against the previous piece. When all of the pieces have been glued and positioned properly, attach steel bar clamps and turn the screws (Figure 5-11).

Figure 5-11:   Bar clamps are used to apply even pressure to the glued hardwood strips. Insert scrap pieces between the clamp and the work to prevent damage.

It is important just prior to applying clamp pressure that you are certain all of the edges are even, the tops are flush and all is ready for the clamping. You should also slip a scrap piece of lumber between the clamp jaw and the edge of the maple stock. Do this at both ends of the clamp. It will protect the maple from being marred by the clamp.

Bar clamps should be spaced at about 12 inches, and alternated, one from one side and one from the other. Begin by turning the screws of one clamp then another until you feel that they are all applying about the same pressure. A small amount of glue should be squeezed from each joint, when the right amount of pressure is applied.

It is important to keep checking the alignment of the maple strips, and you may find a framing square handy for this. If one or more of the pieces is out of line, you can usually persuade it into position by tapping on the end with a wooden mallet or block of wood and hammer.

Once you feel you have about the right amount of pressure, and all the boards are even and square, let the glue set. This will usually take twenty-four hours, but check the glue container label to be sure. No more work can or should be done until the adhesive has dried fully.

Once the glue has set, you can remove the clamps and begin cleaning the face of the counter top. Your first task will be to remove any excess glue along the glue lines. Using a sharp chisel, you should be able to remove any glue spots quickly. Work carefully so you do not gouge the surface with the chisel. Next, you should sand the entire surface to first take down any high areas, and then to make the top smooth. This will entail using different grits of sandpaper from coarse to extra fine.

When the counter top is smooth and flat it can be attached to the counter base. The top is attached from underneath the cabinet, so the screws will not be visible on the finished counter. As you fasten the top to the base, check the surface often with a level to make sure it remains flat. For more details about attaching a counter top to a counter base, see Chapter 10, on "Installation."

After the butcher block type counter top has been securely fastened to the counter base, you can cut a sink hole, if required, and begin applying a finish, if desired. Polyurethane is probably the best clear coating you can apply as it is a very durable finish. If you prefer, however, you can leave the surface natural and simply apply a few coats of paste wax. In either event, your maple strip counter top should provide a lifetime of beautiful service. (See Chapter 9, on "Finishing," for more details on finishes.)

CHAPTER 6

CABINETS

Cabinets are the simplest of all projects in this book to build. They can be either wall mounted, as is most common in the kitchen above the counters, hung from the ceiling, or they can be free standing as in kitchen islands. The difference between a cabinet and a counter is that cabinets do not have drawers. Cabinets either have doors—swing or sliding—or are open-faced. Another distinction of cabinets is that they are storage units with internal shelving.

The U.S. Department of Agriculture has established certain standards for cabinets. Wall cabinets can vary in height depending on the type of installation and distance from the counter. The tops of wall cabinets can be located at the same height, either free or under a 12- to 14-inch drop ceiling or additional storage unit. Wall cabinets are normally 30-inches high, but not more than 21 inches when a range or kitchen sink is located under them. Wall cabinets can also be built in 12, 15, 18 and 24 inch heights. The shorter wall cabinets are usually placed over a refrigerator or wall mounted oven. Narrow cabinets are most commonly built with single doors; wider cabinets have double or sliding doors.

As with counter bases and bathroom vanities, cabinets are nothing more than a box, and this undoubtedly is the reason cabinet building is commonly referred to as "box" construction. Each cabinet will have a top, bottom, two sides, a back and a front. Most of the construction of a cabinet is simple and standard, except for the front of the cabinet, and it is this area that requires the most attention. The back of a wall hung cabinet must, out of necessity, be strong, for the back is the part which is used to attach the cabinet to a wall, unless the unit is hung from the ceiling rafters above.

For smaller size cabinets you do not necessarily have to attach a back which is full size; you can usually make do with two 1 × 4 inch boards set into the back of the cabinet ladder fashion. (Many commercial cabinetmakers use only this back for all their cabinets.) These can then be used to fasten the small cabinet to a finished wall. If, however, the existing wall is in need of repair, or if you are installing the new cabinet on a wall that has only been framed (with no finish covering), you would then have to attach a full back to the cabinet for appearance, as well as insulation.

As mentioned in Chapter 4, "Counter Tops," you might want to cover the newly built cabinet with plastic laminate instead of finishing in some other way. You will have to refer back to Chapter 4 for directions on how to apply this type of finish covering to a surface. The procedures are the same, so there is not much point in duplicating them here.

One of the appealing features about building wall or ceiling hung cabinets is that they can be built and finished in the workshop, then installed in the kitchen. This will enable you to devote more time to the building task and you will not be disrupting the entire household with your project.

In this chapter we will be discussing different types of fronts for cabinets than was discussed in the counter base chapter, Chapter 3. For most cabinets, it is more practical to build a frame out of 1 × 4 or 1 × 6 inch lumber, than it is to cover the front with a piece of plywood and then have to make plunge cuts for the opening. We will also learn how to build slightly different types of doors, such as frame doors, and another type of door which utilizes tongue and groove boards. These can be mounted in the lapped manner as the solid plywood doors discussed in Chapter 3.

Since cabinets have internal shelves, and the various

methods of attaching them are covered in Chapter 3, the reader will not find that information duplicated here. Instead, I will discuss how to make the shelves themselves and only briefly mention the various methods used to attach them to the inside of the cabinet. For a more detailed description, please refer back to Chapter 3.

All of these modifications are adaptable to the counter bases and bathroom vanities covered in Chapter 3.

BUILDING THE BASIC CABINET

As mentioned, a cabinet is simply a box with a front. In fact, if you were to stand an ordinary wooden box on its side, you would, in effect, have a frontless cabinet. Our intention here is to take a simple idea and, using plywood, build a simple cabinet.

Figure 6-1 shows the basic layout for a standard wall hung

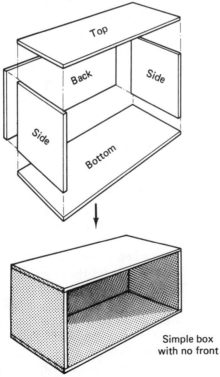

Simple box
with no front

Figure 6-1: A basic wall cabinet design, which can be adapted to most residential needs.

cabinet. Measurements are purposely left out of the diagram so
you can adapt the design to your own specifications. If you are
using ¾-inch plywood, you can make a box about 4 feet long without any center internal supports for the shelf. Greater lengths will
require some type of support, however, even though the shelves
will be supported on three sides (both sides and back), there will
still be a tendency for the shelves to sag with age.

Joints where the top, bottom and back fit together with the
sides can be simple butt joints or, if you want to add greater
strength and test your woodworking skills, you can make dado, or
rabbet joints. Still another type of joint, which has not been discussed in this book, is a doweled butt joint (wooden dowels are
added for additional strength instead of nails).

Doweled Butt Joints

To make a doweled butt joint, you begin the same way as if
you were making a simple butt joint. Before you glue and nail the
pieces together, however, you must make the holes for the dowels.
There are several ways of making these holes and we will discuss
two of them: exposed, and blind or hidden. You will need a marking gauge, electric drill, drill bit the same size as the dowels, some
white glue, dowels and some type of clamping system to hold the
work while drilling the holes. (I use a Black & Decker Workmate.)
Dowels can be purchased at most hardware stores. They are
usually made of maple or birch and come in various diameters
from ¼-inch to ¾-inch in 3 foot lengths.

You should use hardwood dowels for doweled butt joints because of their strength which, incidentally, is greater than finishing nails. Dowels which are made to be used for dowel joints have
ends that are slightly chamfered to prevent binding when they are
forced into place. Also, there is usually a little V-groove cut into
the dowel pin for its entire length, permitting trapped air and glue
to escape from the hole when the dowel is driven into the hole.
This little groove also prevents splitting the pieces of the cabinet
while assembling. The chamfered tips and V-groove are important and should be on every dowel pin you install. If they are not
on the pins you are using, make them yourself using a knife for the
chamfered ends and a saw blade for the V-groove (Figure 6-2).

Begin the process of making dowel holes by dividing the
thickness of the boards you are using in half. Set this measure-
ment on the marking gauge, then scribe the end of one board and
the face of another, where the two pieces will be butted together.

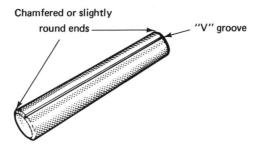

Figure 6-2: Hardwood dowels should be slightly chamfered at both ends and there should be a groove along the side to permit the escape of excess glue.

It is important that the exact center of the end of one board is determined, and once this has been done, the marking gauge will enable you to mark the center of the rest of the cabinet.

Some woodworkers like to carry the center line around the edge of the board to help with alignment when the marks are covered up, and you may want to do this as well.

After I have marked the center line on the face of the outside board, I clamp it and the board which will be its mate together (see Figure 6-3). At this time, I mark the location of the dowel holes on the board which has the center line on its face. Dowel holes should be spaced approximately 4 inches apart.

The next step is to drill the dowel holes. With the proper size drill bit for the size dowels being installed, carefully drill through the face marked board and into the end of the board below. You must hold the drill at a 90 degree angle to the face of the board being drilled. Work carefully. You might find it helpful before you begin drilling to first indent each dowel hole mark with an awl or nail. This center mark or dent will enable you to start drilling in the exact center of the hole.

If you have carefully measured, marked, and drilled the dowel holes, the joint should be perfect. I have found that setting up the work, making sure that the edges are aligned, clamping securely and drilling with care are the best insurance for getting the dowel holes exact.

Sometimes, because the wood you are working with is too thick, or for the sake of appearance, you may not want to see the ends of dowels on the finished cabinet. In cases such as these you will want to construct a blind doweled butt joint, which is, a joint held together with glue and dowel pins but you cannot see them.

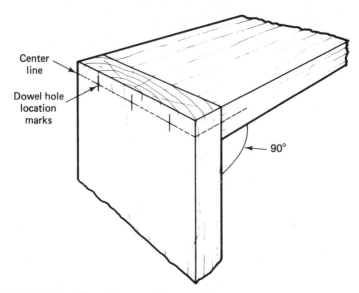

Center
line

Dowel hole
location
marks

← 90°

Figure 6-3: Careful setup for a doweled butt joint is important. You must mark the location of the hole, clamp the pieces securely, and drill at a 90 degree angle to the marks.

The work setup for blind doweled butt joints is very much the same as for the exposed doweled butt joint discussed above. The center of the thickness of the boards is determined and marked on the pieces at the point where they will be joined. Then, instead of clamping the pieces together as they will be joined, they are clamped face to face, with the center marks clearly visible and parallel. Then, using a square, the location of the dowel holes is marked on both pieces (Figure 6-4).

Because the dowel pins are concealed in this type of joint, you only drill part way into each piece, generally half-way. I have found the easiest way to make sure I do not drill too far into each piece is to first determine the depth of the hole and then stick a piece of tape on the drill bit shaft at the depth location. I stop drilling when the piece of tape just touches the work. It is very important, when drilling blind dowel butt joint holes to keep the drill at a perfect 90 degree angle to the marks and work. This will insure that the dowels will line up exactly, but is not an easy task when done freehand unless you have had lots of practice.

There is a tool, a doweling jig, which is designed to help you keep the drill bit at an exact 90 degree angle to the face of the work. Many companies sell doweling jigs so, if you are planning to

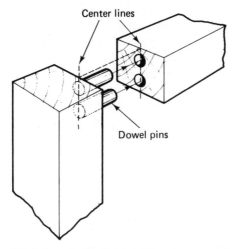

Figure 6-4: A blind doweled butt joint. The pieces are held together by glue and dowels which are internal.

make very many blind doweled butt joints you should consider buying one. A doweling jig is also helpful when making mortise joints.

After the doweled butt joint has been made (either the exposed or blind), you should insert the dowels and fit the pieces together—without glue—and check fit and alignment. If you are satisfied with the joint, take the pieces apart, put a few drops of white glue into each hole, a few drops on each dowel pin, assemble and clamp till the glue sets. The doweled butt joint method of assembly is much stronger and is a bit more challenging than using glue and nails. It is also one way of assembling the face frames and frame doors of the cabinets which will be discussed later in this chapter.

Assemble the cabinet using whichever types of joints you care to try. The bottom is usually attached to the sides first, then the top, and lastly the back is attached to the cabinet. As mentioned earlier in this chapter, you can either attach a full piece of plywood to the back or just two 1 × 4-inch pieces (one along the top and another along the bottom back of the cabinet). Remember that the back of wall hung cabinets serves as the anchor for the rest of the cabinet to the wall studs so if the cabinet you are building is large, use a full back.

A solid back can be either butt jointed to the sides, top and bottom or it can be set flush inside. You may want to rabbet cut

all of the inside back edges of the cabinet for the flush mount.
There are other alternatives—quarter round molding, 1 × 1-inch
stock—and these are discussed in greater detail in Chapter 3.
Please refer to that chapter for more information on cabinet
backs.

If you will be attaching only a partial back to your cabinet
you will have to make ¾ × 3¾-inch cuts to both sides (to accommodate the 1 × 4-inch lumber used as partial back) up from the
bottom and down from the top. For additional strength, you can
tie these back boards to the sides and bottom, as well as the sides
and top pieces (Figure 6-5).

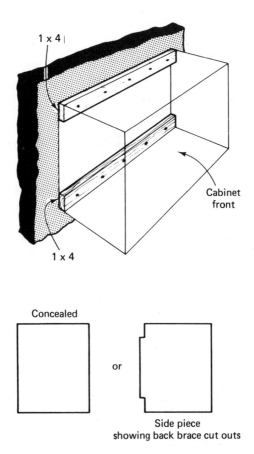

Figure 6-5:   A partial back for a cabinet can consist of two 1 × 4 inch
boards, one attached along the top of the back and the other along the
bottom.

Once the back of the cabinet (either full or partial) has been attached, the cabinet should be fairly rigid and square. The next step is to construct the face of the cabinet.

A face frame is simply a skeletal-like covering for the front of the cabinet. The frame is made from square, clear and straight 1 × 2 or 1 × 4 inch pine or other suitable lumber. It is interesting to note that many of the commercial cabinet, counter and vanity makers now make entire frames out of 1 × 2 inch lumber, then cover these frames with plastic laminate or ¼-inch thick plywood which is then painted.

Since you have already built the cabinet body according to your needs, you will have the dimensions for the front. You should increase these measurements by about 1/16 of an inch to allow for sanding and finishing. The face frame will be fitted over the cabinet front and face nailed or screwed to the sides, top and bottom of the cabinet.

Figure 6-6 shows the basic design for a face frame and you can adopt it for the cabinet(s) you are building. Note that this diagram is for a two door cabinet—that's the reason for the center piece in the frame. If you are planning to have only one door (or more than two) you should make the appropriate modifications to the basic design.

Other Joints

Notice also in Figure 6-6 that there are several different options for joining the pieces. The choices include butt joint with corrugated fasteners (common or commercially made frames), doweled butt joint, lap joint, metal "mending plates" and mortise and tenon joint.

The simplest joint is the common butt joint. The two pieces are placed together and toenailed (with white glue at the junction of the two pieces). This is not the strongest choice of joints but is suitable for small cabinet face frames.

The next simplest way to join two pieces of a face frame involves the use of corrugated fasteners. This method is widely used in commercial cabinet building. The joint itself is actually a butt joint but instead of toenailing, the pieces are joined with corrugated fasteners. You might decide for a different look to miter the two ends (each cut at 45 degree angles) and then join them using corrugated fasteners.

Another butt joint that is commonly used in commercial cabinet building uses a metal plate or strap to secure one piece of the frame to the other. These metal plates form a strong joint and

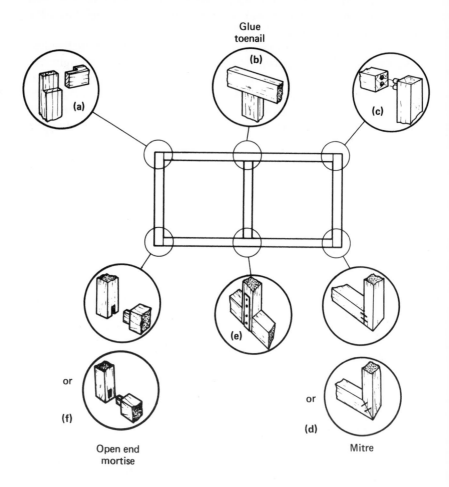

Figure 6-6: Face frame for cabinet showing joint possibilities: (a) lap, (b) butt, (c) doweled, (d) corrugated nails, (e) metal strap, and (f) mortise and tenon.

are simple to attach (with screws) once the pieces have been aligned and positioned properly. Metal brackets come in steel, brass and zinc-plated steel. In most cases these brackets are meant to be concealed but you can create a different type of look by using brass joiners on the face of the cabinet. In addition to straight flat pieces, these brackets are available in a T-shape, L-shape and bent at a 45 degree angle for inside (or outside) corners. It is common practice to add a few of these brackets to the inside of larger cabinets for added strength.

The next type of butt joint is the doweled butt joint and this was discussed earlier in this chapter. Please refer back to that section if you are interested in this type of joint.

The lap joint is another common joint for face framed cabinets, but requires the use of power tools, such as a router or table saw for an accurate fit. A lap joint is simple to make. One half of each of the pieces is removed, and when the pieces are joined, their combined thickness equals the thickness of a single, uncut piece of lumber. This is a strong joint which has a good appearance, and it is not difficult to make.

The last joint in the illustration is the mortise and tenon. It is a difficult joint to make by hand, especially when using 1 × 2 or 1 × 4 inch stock, and is therefore not recommended unless you are interested in a time consuming challenge.

The mortise is the hole and the tenon is the projection on the adjoining piece. Of the two, the mortise is the harder to make as it must be done, at least in part, with a chisel. You can drill out most of the mortise first and then square the inside off using a chisel.

Then the tenon is cut on the end of the adjoining piece. While a tenon can be made with a handsaw or chisel, it is easier (and the tenon will be more accurate) if it is done on a table saw or with a router.

After both the mortise and tenon have been cut they should be tried for fit, and any adjustments made before gluing and clamping.

One variation of this joint, and one that is a bit easier to construct is called the open mortise and tenon or slip joint. A slip joint is very much like a mortise and tenon joint except that one end of the mortise is removed. This entire joint can be easily created using a table saw, and is actually better suited for corners of face frames and is widely used commercially.

Assemble the face frame using whichever joints you feel will be the easiest for you to work with. Keep in mind that the frame must be strong, for the doors will land on it. Care should be exercised wherever two parts of the frame join—the angle must be a perfect 90 degrees. You can be fairly certain of this angle if all the end cuts which you must make are square. Carefully mark the cuts using a pencil and tri-square, then make exact cuts (Figure 6-7).

While assembling the face frame with corrugated nails, or metal straps, make sure that the finished side, the side that will be facing outward from the finished cabinet, is down and you are fastening from the back of the frame.

Figure 6-7:   Use a square and pencil to mark the frame pieces before cutting for it is important to have squarely cut ends.

Once the face frame has been constructed, you can attach it to the front of the cabinet. The frame is commonly face nailed onto the cabinet after a bead of white glue has been put over all contacting surfaces and the frame has been positioned properly. Options to face nailing include countersunk screws (fill the resultant holes with either wood putty, spackle or with wood plugs which have been glued in place) and wooden dowel pins, suitably glued. After the face frame has been attached to the front of the cabinet, you can attach the doors.

CABINET DOORS

As mentioned earlier in this chapter, we will be discussing a few variations to the standard plywood, overlapping door which was covered in Chapter 3. If you are interested in making solid doors from plywood, remember that the door must be wider than the opening, and that is about the only requirement. Alternatives to solid plywood doors include: hollow core doors, frame doors, plank doors and variations of these. While most of these doors are lighter than plywood equivalents, there is a bit more work involved in their construction. One other alternative,which I did not mention, is ready-made doors. Most lumber yards or building supply houses across the country usually stock cabinet doors in standard sizes (odd sizes have to be specially ordered) so this is surely one way to go, especially if you want some fancy type scroll work which would be almost impossible to create using hand or small shop tools.

Since the point of this book is to explain how to build your own cabinets, counters and vanities, we can leave the stock doors and other millwork for other folks.

One very simple type of door to build is a hollow core door. Simply a frame—commonly 1 × 1 inch square lumber covered with ¼-inch plywood or plastic laminate (see Figure 6-8). It should be noted that narrow hollow core doors have a four piece frame, while doors that are wider (18 inches) or higher (over 24 inches) should have a center strip. For the record, this center piece is called a stile.

Hollow core door frame

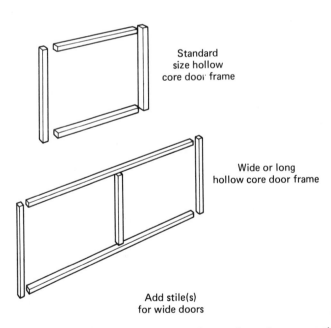

Standard
size hollow
core door frame

Wide or long
hollow core door frame

Add stile(s)
for wide doors

Figure 6-8: The frame for hollow core frame doors is commonly built from 1 × 1 inch stock then covered with ¼-inch plywood or plastic laminate.

Use any suitable joint system for constructing the frame then cover it with ¼-inch plywood. If you do not want to have nail or screw heads visible on the finished door, consider gluing the plywood to the frame instead of nailing or screwing. White or hide glue is suitable for this, as the door itself will not be that heavy. Glue the pieces, then clamp or weigh down until the glue sets.

For hardware you can either attach a knob, handle or rout out a notch along the bottom edge of the door as a finger pull.

One variation of the plywood covering for this type of door is to cover the frame with plastic laminate. As discussed in Chapter 4, use contact cement to attach the laminate to the frame.

Another type door—a frame door—is in some ways similar to an ordinary picture frame, but has the addition of a back of some type. This type of door has a basic design upon which you can create some interesting, custom looking doors.

Begin by building a four-sided frame using 1 × 2 inch or 1 × 4 inch wide, clear pine or other suitable lumber. The four corner joints can be the simple butt type or any of the other possibilities discussed earlier in this chapter (see face frames). Most commercial cabinet doors utilize a slip joint for all corners. Before assembling the frame, however, you may want to add some type of decorative edge to the inside edges of the frame.

The easiest and most precise way of adding a decorative touch to the inside of frame doors is with a router and special bit. There are many different types of decorative bits for routers, as Figure 6-9 illustrates. Bear in mind, however, that adding a custom edge to the doors will be much easier to accomplish if this work is done before the door frame is assembled.

Another task which must be done before the door is assembled is to rabbet cut the inside back edge of the door. This is done so the plywood (or other material) back can be attached flush to the back of the frame. Most frame door backs are ¼-inch thick plywood, so the depth of the rabbet cut will also be ¼-inch deep. Then, when the door is assembled, the back simply fits flush into place.

The material for the back of the door is commonly ¼-inch thick plywood, but you can use other materials for a different look. One example is clear or tinted glass or a textured opaque plastic. The advantage of plastic is that it is not heavy and it is also unbreakable. Home improvement centers sell many different types of decorative panels, some are the metal mesh type, while others are specially textured ¼-inch plywood. You might also consider purchasing a panel of ¼-inch thick plywood with a hardwood

Frame doors

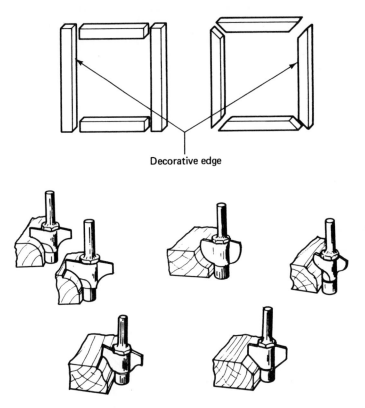

Decorative edge

Figure 6-9: Frame cabinet doors are lightweight, simple to construct, and functional. Consider finishing off the inside edge with a special router bit. Build the frame with simple butt joints, mitre joints or other joints, as discussed in the text.

veneer face. The possibilities are limited only by your imagination when it comes to frame doors, so look at what is available when planning this construction project.

The last type of door we will discuss in this section utilizes 1 × 4, 1 × 6, and 1 × 8 inch tongue and grooved boards. For this type of door, you can use either all one size lumber or combinations to arrive at the required width. This type of door is simple to build but is heavier than any other type of door discussed in this book. It is actually more suited for a cabinet which will get a lot of use and that is taller than wide e.g., a broom cabinet. The appearance of the finished door is also on the rustic side.

Construction is simple; the proper number of boards are fastened together, tongue to groove, until the required width is attained. Then, while making sure that the door remains square, other boards (usually 1 × 2 inch clear lumber) are attached in a "Z" configuration across the face to the door as in Figure 6-10. These face boards will be visible on the finished door and serve to add strength to the door as they are screwed into place. A little planning is called for here when using the "Z" face pattern so when the cabinet is viewed in conjunction with other cabinets (with the same "Z") all is in balance. One variation is an "X" pattern.

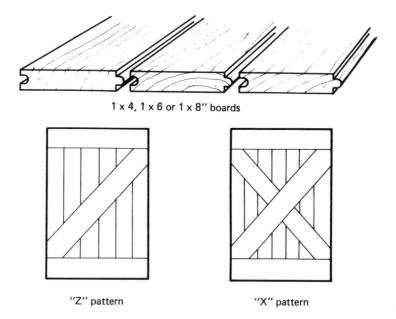

1 x 4, 1 x 6 or 1 x 8" boards

"Z" pattern   "X" pattern

Figure 6-10: A simple but attractive cabinet door can be constructed with tongue and groove boards. Strength comes from the cross pieces, which are screwed into place.

The edges of these doors can be left as is, or the groove can be cut off one side and the tongue off the other. If cutting and the resultant square edges are desired, this should be done to the two outer boards before the face boards are attached.

Tongue and groove doors can be either flush or lap mounted. If they are to be flush mounted, keep this in mind while making them as they will have to fit inside the opening in the cabinet. If they are to be lap mounted, they should be one inch larger all around the opening. See Chapter 8 for a discussion on hardware.

INTERNAL SHELVING

As mentioned earlier in this chapter, the main difference between a counter base and cabinet is that the former has both drawers and shelves while the latter only has shelves. The ways in which internal shelving can be suspended inside a cabinet or counter are discussed thoroughly in Chapter 3, and you should refer back to that chapter for actual installation instructions. You may remember that there are three ways which we discussed: shelf supports, cleats and dado cuts in the internal walls into which the shelves fit (Figure 6-11).

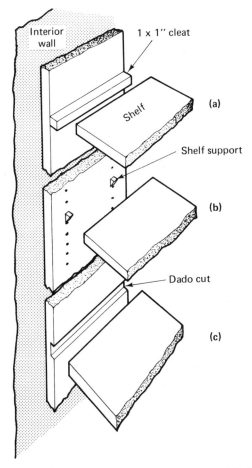

Figure 6-11:   Internal shelves can be suspended by (a) cleats, (b) shelf supports, or (c) dado grooves in the cabinet wall.

The material that the shelves themselves are made from can be any one or combination of plywood, particle board or 1-inch thick lumber (1 × 8 or 1 × 10 inch for example).

The simplest type of shelves are particle board shelves. In fact, many lumber yards now stock particle board that is precut to standard shelf widths. I find these type of shelves very easy to use but certainly not the most attractive choice for shelving material.

You can use ⅝- or ¾-inch thick plywood cut to the proper width and length for your internal shelves. Remember, however, that you will have to fill the exposed edges of these shelves for appearance sake, and this involves not only filling, but finish sanding as well. Still, plywood shelves are functional and relatively inexpensive.

One other alternative is to use 1-inch thick boards for internal shelving. Good choices are 1 × 8, 1 × 10 and 1 × 12 inch clear pine, cedar or redwood boards. When you use these type of boards for shelving material you have a chance to do something decorative to the edges that face out of the cabinet. Consider using a special router bit to create a custom look to your shelf edges (Figure 6-12).

(Courtesy of Black & Decker)

Figure 6-12:   Add a decorative touch to the edges of your shelves by using a router and special bit.

After you have built the cabinet, attached the doors, installed the internal shelving, and finished the unit (see Chapter 9, "Finishing"), you will want to attach the cabinet to an existing wall. This will usually involve the use of toggle bolts or some other means of solidly attaching the cabinet, through its back to the wall. For more information on how to attach hanging cabinets to an interior wall or ceiling, please see Chapter 10, which is all about installation of cabinets, counters and vanities.

CHAPTER 7

DRAWERS

While it is entirely possible to find kitchen counters, cabinets and bathroom vanities without drawers, the majority of the units you will find will have drawers. Drawers not only expand the overall storage capacity of counter and cabinets, they also help you to more effectively organize the kitchen.

Lumberyards sell ready-made drawers in standard sizes, but in about the same amount of time it will take you to drive to the yard, pick out what you require and drive back home, you can custom make your own drawers. Simple, functional drawers can be made with just an electric hand-held saw, hammer, nails and glue. Slightly more intricate drawers can be made using a stationary saw or hand-held router. Depending on your woodworking skills and the tools you have available, not to mention your design requirements, you should have no problem making your own custom drawers, since all drawer construction is basically the same: front, sides, back and bottom (Figure 7-1).

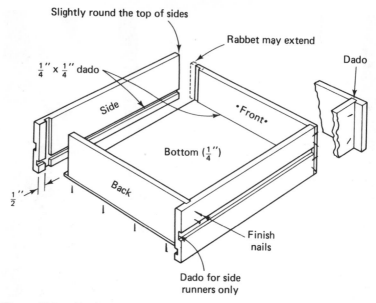

Slightly round the top of sides

Rabbet may extend

Dado

$\frac{1}{4}''$ x $\frac{1}{4}''$ dado

Side

•Front•

Bottom ($\frac{1}{4}''$)

Back

$\frac{1}{2}''$

Finish
nails

Dado for side
runners only

Figure 7-1:   Exploded view of basic drawer design.

There are two basic systems which enable drawers to slide properly: wooden or built-in slide guides and metal drawer hardware or sliders. Wooden slide guides require a bit more planning and construction, and tend to work less efficiently than metal drawer hardware. In addition, metal drawer hardware is very simple to install and will work like a charm for the life of the unit. The latter part of this chapter will cover the types of guidance systems that you can build as well as the sliding systems that are ready-made.

Although the basic design of all drawers is the same, the one area where there can be a major difference is the face of the drawer. Basically, there are two types of drawer front designs: flush or lip. A flush drawer fits into the front of the counter or cabinet and, when closed, reveals the outline of the drawer opening. Flush drawers, while not really difficult to construct, do require a bit more work to make and fit properly (Figure 7-2).

Lip drawers, as the name indicates, have a face that comes to rest on the front of the counter or cabinet. When a lip drawer is closed, you cannot see the outline of the drawer opening because the face of the drawer is actually larger, all around, than that opening. Lip drawers are easier to construct than flush drawers, and therefore are recommended for the do-it-yourselfer. In my

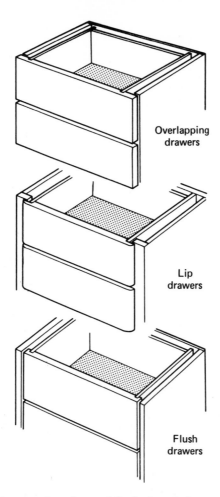

Figure 7-2: Overlapping, lip, and flush drawer types.

opinion, flush drawers require more work than is necessary for a utilitarian drawer system and therefore should be used in only the more specialized counters and cabinets. I always build lip drawers because I prefer the ease with which they can be constructed and, frankly, I like the way they look.

Another area where there is some room for deviation in drawer construction is in the side joints of the drawer, that is; where the sides join the front and back of the drawer. The drawer joint area can be any one, or combination of several joints: butt, dado, rabbet, or dovetail (see Figure 7-3). A brief discussion of these joints follows.

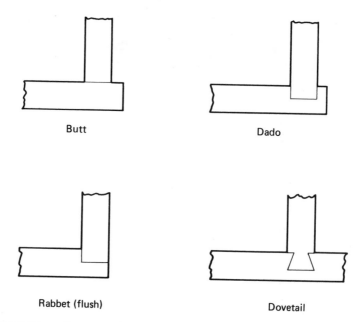

Figure 7-3:   Common drawer joints.

Butt Joints

Butt joints are without a doubt the simplest of all joints to construct. Butt joints are made by placing the ends of the drawer sides against the back of the face of the drawer. Nails are then driven through the face of the drawer and into the end of the side. A few drops of white glue between the pieces will add greater strength to this joint. Butt joints are not the best choice for drawer construction because not only will the nail heads or filled holes be visible, but the strength of the drawer is less than if one of the other joints is used instead.

You can add strength and a touch of utilitarian class to drawers with simple butt joints by using countersunk brass wood screws instead of nails. Drawers put together in this fashion are attractive and distinct, especially if the face of the drawer is either a special wood, such as white oak, or if the finish is left natural, but protected by a coating of clear varnish or polyurethane.

Dado Joints

A dado is simply a groove cut across the grain of a board. In this case, the back of the face of the drawer. It is into this groove that the ends of the sides are fitted when assembling the drawer.

To lay out the work for making a dado cut, place the front of the drawer face down, and position the end of the side where you want it ultimately to be. Scribe this location with a marking tool or pencil, remove the side, then check the squareness of the marking with a square. Then, make the dado cut.

I have found that the easiest way to make dado cuts is with a hand-held router, but this cut can be made on a stationary table saw or even with a hand-held circular saw. Whichever tool you choose for making the dado cut, remember that setting up for the cut is 95 percent of the work, so extreme care must be exercised.

The depth of the dado cut, assuming that the face of the drawer is ¾-inch plywood, is ⅜- to ½-inch deep.

Rabbet Joints

A rabbet is a recess cut out of an edge of a piece of wood. It is similar to the dado cut except that it is made on the end of a piece of lumber rather than along the surface. The bottom of a rabbet cut is parallel to the face of the drawer and the side is parallel to the end or edge. The rabbet cut is commonly used (as is the dado) wherever the end grain of the wood is to be concealed.

As with the dado cut, the rabbet cut can be made with either stationary or portable tools. I prefer to use a hand-held router because it is quicker and produces a nicer edge than a saw, either table or hand-held.

The depth of a rabbet cut, on the back of the drawer front is ⅜ to ½ inch, assuming of course that the drawer front is ¾-inch stock.

Dovetail Joints

Look at any fine piece of furniture with drawers and chances are 99 out of 100 that the drawer joints will be dovetailed. Dovetail joints are about the strongest of all joints because the sides and front of the drawer are actually interlocked. As is to be expected, dovetail joints are difficult to make and should only be used where great strength and beauty are to be combined.

While dovetail joints can be made by hand, this is a process that can take more time than you may be willing to spend. The best tool for making a dovetail joint is a router with a special jig and template. This setup will greatly simplify making dovetail joints, and is comparatively easy to master, once you have become proficient at setting up the jig and template (Figure 7-4).

Figure 7-4: The dovetail drawer joint is most easily made with a router and special dovetail template.

Drawer Bottoms

Drawer bottoms are most commonly made from ¼-inch thick plywood or masonite. There are two methods currently used to attach the drawer bottom to the drawer: flush mounted or set into a dado groove (Figure 7-5).

The flush mount for the drawer bottom is the simplest because you simply measure the drawer, cut a piece of ¼-inch ply-

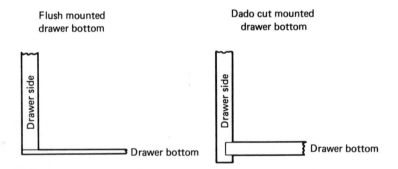

Figure 7-5: Section views of two ways to mount drawer bottom to sides, front and back of drawer.

wood, then glue and nail the bottom to the front, sides and back of the drawer. There can be variations here, especially if the drawer front is of the lip type.

One variation of the flush mounted drawer bottom is to extend the edges of the bottom and use them as the guidance system for the drawer, as in Figure 7-7.

The drawer bottom that is fitted into a dado cut requires more time to make because of the extra cuts involved, but this type of drawer bottom is much stronger than the type which is simply fastened to the bottom of the drawer. Dado cuts must be made along both sides, usually ½ to 1 inch up from the bottom, across the back of the drawer front and possibly along the back of the drawer. It is not uncommon, however, to simply make dado cuts along both sides and not the front or back. The theory being here that the support the bottom will receive from the sides is more than adequate.

DRAWER GUIDANCE SYSTEMS

As mentioned earlier in this chapter, there are two basic ways to guide a drawer and make it slide: the built-in system and metal drawer hardware. Since the built-in drawer guides require more work, we will discuss them first.

If the drawer is small, you can usually slide it in the box-like enclosure which is the cabinet housing or frame, but for larger drawers you will need some type of guidance system to prevent the drawer from binding as it is pulled out or pushed back into the cabinet. Built-in guidance systems can be in either of two places: the sides or bottom of the drawer and cabinet. Side guides work well for most types of drawers because the weight of the drawer is spread out over both sides. Bottom (or center guides as they are sometimes referred to) must be mounted on the frame of the cabinet, and therefore there must be some support along the sides for the weight of the drawer. Bottom guides require more internal framing, more space between the drawers, and are not the best choice of a built-in guidance system. Bottom guides are most commonly used on very wide drawers.

Figure 7-6 illustrates some of the possible drawer guidance systems that you can build into the cabinet. The simplest to build are those that are simply strips of ½ × ½ inch hardwood stock, which have been attached to the internal sides of the cabinet. The drawer rests on these strips and can be slid in or out easily. In some applications this system is a poor choice because there is

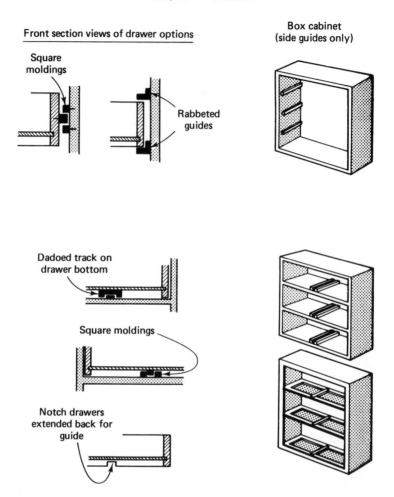

Figure 7-6:   Built-in drawer guidance systems.

nothing to keep the drawer from being pulled entirely out of the guides.

Another alternative is to rabbet cut guides from 1 inch square hardwood stock, such as oak, and then attach these guides to the interior walls of the cabinet.

Still another guidance system can be constructed by making a dado cut along the internal wall of the cabinet. Then, you can attach a hardwood runner to the side of the drawer. This is a good choice of guidance systems because the weight of the drawer is supported by the hardwood strip. The most practical way to attach this hardwood strip is with white glue and screws. For trouble free operation, countersink the screw heads.

One other drawer guidance system involves the use of the bottom itself. The internal walls of the cabinet are first dado cut at a predetermined distance to receive the drawer bottom. The bottom of the drawer (plywood) is cut wider than the width of the drawer, and then either glued and nailed or glued and screwed to the bottom of the drawer frame. Now the drawer bottom is part of the guidance system. If you decide to use this system use ½-inch rather than ¼-inch thick plywood for the drawer bottom. This will not only make for a stronger drawer, but will insure a long life for the guidance system (Figure 7-7).

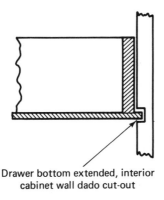

Drawer bottom extended, interior
cabinet wall dado cut-out

Figure 7-7:   Drawer bottom guidance system.

For trouble free service from any of the built-in drawer guidance systems there are a few things you should do to the drawers. Before the drawers are pressed into service you should first coat all parts of the guidance system with a wood sealer. Then you should either paint them with an oil base glossy enamel or shellac, and after the finish has dried, wax or lubricate the guides. There are several types of spray-on lubricants for drawers. Application of a finish coating and lubricant will insure that your wooden drawer guidance system works well for a long time.

Metal drawer hardware, sometimes referred to as "drawer slides," are the modern way to have drawers that slide easily. Your local hardware or lumberyard should have a selection of these in stock as they have become quite popular.

There are two basic types of drawer hardware available; those that support and guide the drawer by its sides and those that support and guide the drawer from the bottom. In addition, drawer hardware can be either the full or partial extension type. The basic difference here is in how far the drawer can be pulled out before it is stopped by the drawer hardware. Obviously, full extension hardware lets you pull the drawer out to its full length, while the partial extension type of hardware will let the drawer be pulled out only part of its length. The basic difference between these two types of drawer hardware is the number of pieces in the sliding system.

The full extension type of drawer hardware is a three piece unit. One piece attaches to the drawer side, there is a middle telescoping member, and a third piece is attached to the internal frame of the cabinet.

Partial extension drawer hardware is commonly two pieces; one is attached to the drawer sides and the other to the internal wall of the cabinet or counter. This type of drawer hardware is less expensive, and more prone to problems (if the load is heavy) than the full extension drawer hardware.

Generally speaking, I prefer the full extension type of drawer hardware because it is practically trouble-free and, as the name implies, the drawer can be pulled out to its full length.

Since drawer hardware manufacturers supply complete instructions for installing their sliders in a cabinet, there is little need to duplicate those directions here. A few general comments can be made, however, about drawer hardware.

Drawer hardware is rated as either light, medium, or heavy duty—25–50, 75–100, and 150 pound range respectively. Some manufacturers make an extra heavy duty drawer sliding system that can handle loads up to about 250 pounds or so, but these usually have to be special ordered. When buying drawer hardware, estimate the maximum number of pounds the drawer will hold, and buy the sliding system that comes the closest. There is little need to get the heavier drawer hardware for, say a silverware drawer, as the heavier the hardware the higher the cost.

Before building the drawers for your counter, buy the drawer hardware. The reason for doing this is that most manufacturers will be quite specific as to clearances between the drawer and hardware. In most cases, for example, the hardware and drawer will not work properly if there is a variance of over 1/16 of an inch. Needless to say, it is imperative to follow the manufacturer's instructions to the letter for predictable results and good service from the drawer hardware.

Another reason for buying the slide hardware before building the drawer is so you will know the minimum height the drawer must be. In no case can the drawer height be less than the height of the drawer hardware. Drawer hardware ranges in height from about 1¼ inch to about 4 inches, depending on maker, type and capacity.

Drawer hardware, generally speaking, is available in standard lengths from 12 to 30 inches, in 2-inch increments (some makers will supply these in 1-inch increments). In some areas of the country you can also special order nonstandard lengths for odd length drawers.

While shopping for sliding drawer hardware check out some of the special features offered by some makers. Some types of drawer hardware are "nonhanded," that is, they can be used on either the left or right sides of the drawer. Other special features might include adjustable stops, brackets for mounting the drawer (which might mean that internal partitions can be eliminated), positive locking systems, quick release mechanisms, and other special features.

Keep in mind if you decide to use metal drawer hardware, that the internal size of the drawer will be slightly smaller than if you were to build some type of guidance system into the cabinet or counter. This is because the drawer hardware must be installed either between the sides of the drawer and the counter, or along the bottom of the drawer. Arguments in favor of metal drawer hardware include the fact that there are no problems with humidity changes, heavy loads are no problem (if you use the proper size hardware), and providing you choose the full extension type of hardware, you will be able to pull the drawer out to its full length. As far as I am concerned, metal drawer hardware is the best choice for drawers that get opened and closed often.

The last point to discuss about drawers is how they are pulled out—that is knobs, drawer pulls, invisible drawer pulls and design pulls. Since the next chapter discusses all types of hardware from hinges to drawer pulls, there is little need to duplicate that information here, but I would like to point out some of the alternatives to conventional drawer hardware.

The first alternative to drawer pulls and related hardware are "invisible" drawer pulls. By invisible I mean that at first glance there appears to be no conventional knob or drawer pull; the face of the drawer is flat and free of any hardware. There is really no magic here, instead, a rabbet cut is made along the bottom edge of the drawer and serves as a pull for the entire length of the drawer. You will see this type of drawer pull on many of the modern, ready-made or custom kitchen counter drawers as well as on modern bathroom vanities. Figure 7-8 illustrates the invisible drawer pull.

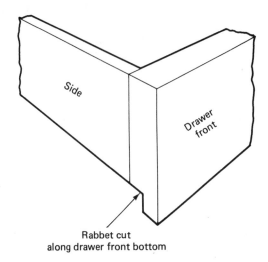

Rabbet cut
along drawer front bottom

Figure 7-8:   Invisible drawer pull—a simple rabbet cut.

Invisible drawer pulls are not only contemporary, and clever, they are practical as well. If you have children, for example there is little chance that a child can be injured as a result of invisible hardware. In addition, there are no handholds for small hands if a child attempts to climb up on kitchen counters. One other point in favor of invisible drawer pulls is that the face of the drawer is easy to keep clean. Conventional hardware (and the area around it) seem to be a target for dirt and soiled hands.

Another type of drawer hardware, which is becoming very popular in modern American homes, is that which is actually part of the design of the counter, cabinet or vanity.

In most cases, design drawer pulls are simply cuts made to the face of the drawer. Cuts, usually 3 to 4 inches long and 1½ to 2 inches high, are made along the top center of the drawer face. There is actually no drawer hardware, as such, but simply a slot in the drawer face, large enough to stick a few fingers. This is how design drawer pulls work.

Variations are possible and limited only by your imagination and the overall design of the counter or cabinet. As Figure 7-9 illustrates, you can make an oval cut along the top of the drawer, or a square cut, or one or more holes. Give these types of drawer pulls some thought while planning your building project and you may come up with a drawer pull design that is more suitable than conventional knobs and handles.

To make these kinds of cuts you can use a coping saw, sabre

saw or a band saw. In most cases, the overall look will be more effective if the cut out is centered on the face of the drawer, either along the top edge or slightly below. As a finishing touch you should sand the edges of the inside of the cut and fill the edges with a suitable edge filler. For more information about finishing, see Chapter 9.

Drawer front views

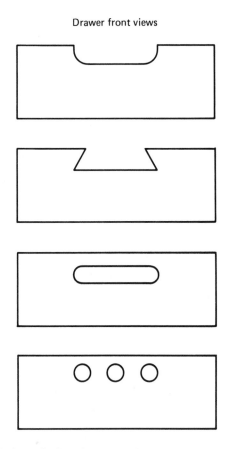

Figure 7-9:   Various design drawer pulls.

CHAPTER 8

HARDWARE

Just one visit to your local hardware store or home improvement center will be enough to convince you that there is a vast array of cabinet hardware available. If any further proof is needed, thumb through any of the woodworking periodicals (such as *How-To, Handyman,* or *Woodworker*) and you will see advertisement after advertisement for not only various types of hardware, but entire catalogs listing thousands of different hinges, knobs, pulls, catches, and anything else you can imagine that might be related to cabinet hardware. Selecting cabinet hardware need not be at all difficult once you know some of the basics.

HINGES

There are five basic types of hinges that fall into the general category of cabinet hardware; butt, offset, flush, invisible, and pivot. The type of hinges you choose will, at least in part, depend on the type of doors you are planning to have on your cabinet; flush doors for example, can use a few different types of hinges while lapped doors are limited to offset hinges.

Butt hinges are probably the most widely used type of hinges in the world. One common example of a butt hinge can be found on most front doors in America. Butt hinges come in all shapes, sizes, styles and finishes. They can be mounted on flush fitting doors so that only the hinge pin is visible or, if a decorative style is chosen, they can be mounted on the face of both the door and cabinet (Figure 8-1).

If you build a cabinet with flush fitting doors, you may decide that you do not want to have the face of the cabinet cluttered with hinge hardware. In this case you can install butt hinges between the cabinet frame and the door edge. There are several ways of doing this: you can mortise the thickness of one hinge leaf onto both the door and cabinet frame; mortise only one side, or you can mount the hinge on top of the edge of both the cabinet frame and door. Keep in mind, however, that if you mortise both

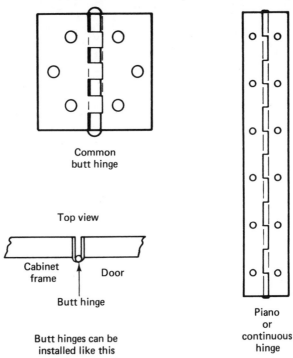

Common
butt hinge

Top view

Cabinet
frame   Door

Butt hinge

Butt hinges can be
installed like this

Piano
or
continuous
hinge

Figure 8-1:   Butt hinges are probably the most widely used of all the hinge types. Above are a few examples.

sides of the hinge seat the space between the door and frame will
be very thin, making the door appear as if it were part of the
cabinet, but if you simply mount the hinge on the edge of the door
and frame, the gap between the door and frame will be the thickness of the hinge. In other words, the mortise reduces the gap between the door and cabinet frame.

To install butt hinges in a flush mounted door you should
begin by putting the door into the cabinet. You will have to prop
the door in place for at this time there is nothing holding the door.
You should leave a small gap between the door and frame. This
can most easily be accomplished by inserting a paper match, or
the equivalent, between the door and frame. Next, mark the location of the hinges on both the edge of the cabinet and the edge of
the frame. Then remove the door and cut the mortise.

Since the leaves of cabinet butt hinges are not very thick,
you can make the mortise cuts with a sharp utility knife. Begin by
outlining the location of the hinge with the knife, then remove the
waste wood with a sharp chisel. Slip one leaf of the hinge into the
mortise and check for fit; the face of the hinge should be flush with
the edge of the door. Next, the cabinet frame receives the same
treatment.

After both the door and cabinet frame have been mortised,
and you are satisfied with the fit, attach one leaf of the hinge to
the door edge, lift the door into its proper position on the cabinet
and screw the other half of the hinge into its mortise. Of course,
you will be installing at least two butt hinges for every door,
spaced about 2½ feet apart.

All butt hinges are installed in the same manner, but some
are easier than others. Loose pin butt hinges, for example, are installed as described above except that one leaf is installed on the
door, and the other half on the frame, then the door is lifted into
place, the hinges meshed, and a pin dropped into place. Loose pin
butt hinges are very easy to install especially for large doors, as
you do not have to hold the door while attaching the other half of
the hinge to the cabinet frame.

Other types of butt hinges are installed directly to the face of
the cabinet and door. There are many different types of decorative butt hinges for this type of mounting but remember they can
only be used when the doors are flush fitting.

Offset hinges are, essentially, butt hinges and they are available for several different types of installations. Offset hinges are
available in semiconcealed and surface mounted styles (Figure
8-2). Offset hinges find the greatest use, however, when the doors

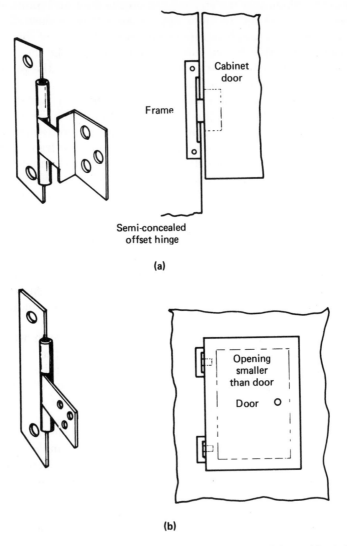

Figure 8-2: Offset hinges are most commonly used for cabinet doors which are larger than the opening; lapped are also available for flush mounted doors.

of the cabinet are mounted so they overlap the frame, as discussed in Chapter 6.

Installing offset hinges is a simple process providing you purchase the right size hinges. Keep in mind when shopping for offset hinges that the amount of the offset must be equal to the thickness of the door. Directions for mounting are usually included in each package of two offset hinges.

Flush hinges are probably the simplest of all the types of hinges to install, as they are mounted on the face of flush fitting doors and to the face of the cabinet. The only difficulty you may encounter is in choosing the type of flush hinges for your cabinet as there are many different styles, sizes and finishes.

Flush hinges are actully butt hinges (see Figure 8-3), but are intended to be a form of decoration for the cabinet as well as being the means by which the cabinet can be opened and closed.

Installation is simple. First, position the door in the cabinet—the door must be flush mounted—mark the location of the hinge on both the door and cabinet, drill screw holes, then screw the hinge into place.

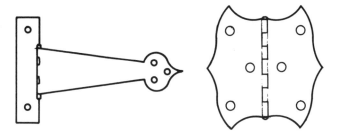

Figure 8-3: Flush hinges are the simplest of all hinges to install.

Pivot hinges are available for both flush mounted and overlapping doors, and there are three basic types: those that attach to the top and bottom edges of the door; those that attach to the vertical edge of the door; and, "knife" hinges which also attach to the top and bottom of the door. One, very appealing feature of pivot hinges is that only the small pivot of the hinge is visible after the cabinet door has been installed.

The last type of hinge, the invisible hinge, requires more than the average amount of woodworking experience to install. Invisible hinges are undoubtedly the most expensive of all hinges and, therefore should be used in only the finest cabinets. When an invisible hinge has been installed properly it is, indeed, invisible when the cabinet door is closed. Invisible hinges are available for both flush mounted and overlapped doors. Instructions and a template should be included with each pair of these hinges.

KNOBS, HANDLES AND CATCHES

The main purpose of a knob or handle is to make it easier to open or close doors and drawers. If this were the only requirement there would be a lot fewer knobs and handles for sale in hardware stores and home improvement centers. Presently offered for sale are knobs and handles made from wood, plastic, steel, aluminum, porcelain, and other materials (Figure 8-4). The design and general look of the cabinet is also a consideration (probably more important than function) when choosing the right type of handles and knobs for your cabinets.

Add to the vast array of ready-made knobs and handles the ones you can make in your workshop (as well as those discussed in Chapter 3) and the possibilities are limitless. Keep in mind while shopping for knobs and handles, the overall design of the storage unit and ask yourself how the particular knob you are considering will look on the finished cabinet (Figure 8-5).

If you would like to make your own knobs and handles, here are some suggestions: a block of hardwood 1 × 2 inches thick, by

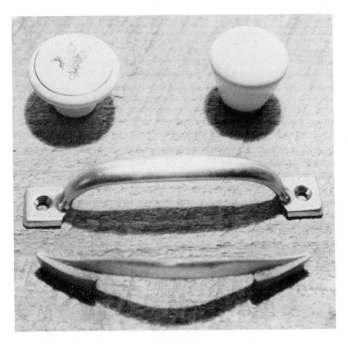

Figure 8-4:   Just a few of the many different types of knobs and handles available.

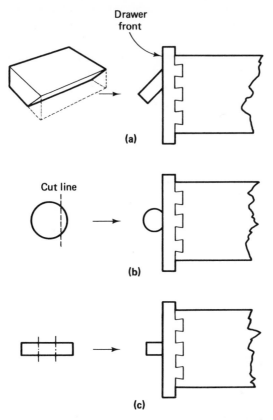

Figure 8-5: Drawer handles and pulls can also be made in the home workshop: (a) hardwood block, (b) dowel with a flat edge, and (c) dowel attached on end.

4 inches long, with one edge bevel cut. Screw this drawer pull onto the face of the drawer from the inside of the drawer.

A 4-inch long piece of 1½–2 inch in diameter wooden dowel with one edge cut flat, can be screwed horizontally to the face of a drawer for an attractive and functional drawer pull.

A 1½–2 inch diameter dowel, cut to about 2 inches in length, can be fastened to the face of a drawer (from the back of the drawer) for a simple but effective drawer pull.

Whether you decide to buy or make knobs and handles just keep in mind the design of the storage unit. You should not attach any hardware to drawers or doors until they have been painted or otherwise finished. This will make the finishing easier and also avoid getting any of the finish coating on the knob or handle.

Most cabinet doors have some type of catch system to keep the door closed. These can be the roller type, friction, or magnetic type.

All catches are installed in about the same manner. The holding mechanism (friction roller or magnet) is most commonly mounted on the cabinet and the strike plate or finger (which fits between the roller or friction mechanism) is mounted on the door.

By far, the most popular type of catch is the magnetic catch (Figure 8-6). These are easy to install and seem to work for a life-time with no problem whatsoever. Magnetic catches can be mounted anywhere on the face frame of the cabinet as long as the steel plate (which is attached to the door) comes into contact when the door is closed. There are several different sizes of magnetic catches but the smaller ones are, generally speaking, the best type to choose, as they will keep most cabinet doors closed and enable you to open the door with little effort. Some of the larger magnetic catches, on the other hand, will cause the cabinet door to slam and make you use two hands to open it.

Figure 8-6:   Magnetic door catches are the most popular and are very simple to install.

You may want to add a piece or two of felt to either the back of the cabinet door or the face of the cabinet (where the two meet) to soften the shock of closing the door. In addition, a small piece of felt will serve to eliminate any marring of the two surfaces.

Cabinet hardware performs a dual function, therefore it is important that you plan the type of hardware almost as carefully as you plan the cabinet building project. This will insure that your cabinets work just as good as they look.

CHAPTER 9

FINISHING

Once kitchen counters, cabinets, and bathroom vanities have been constructed, the final step is to finish them with some form of protective coating. Of course, counter tops that have been covered with plastic laminate will not require any additional protection, nor will other parts of cabinets which have been covered in this way. But for all practical purposes there will be some painting involved for every storage unit you build. Insides for example, must be protected with some type of coating.

Since just about every project described in this book uses plywood (in some form) as a major construction material, the ways in whch you approach finishing will be similiar. Differences will occur, of course, depending on the type of finish you want. The choices are: painting with solid colors; clear finishes (varnish, shellac, polyurethane); stains; and waxes. This chapter will discuss these finishes and how to apply them. However, before we can discuss how to finish a cabinet, counter or vanity, surface preparation must be covered. You cannot expect to obtain professional looking (and enduring) results with finishes applied to a poorly prepared surface. By most estimates, surface preparation is 90 percent of the finishing process.

Before we get into actual surface preparation, I'd like to mention the materials and tools necessary for finishing.

MATERIALS, TOOLS AND FINISH COATINGS

Although most people refer to abrasives as "sandpaper" there is actually no sand on them. There are four types of abrasives used in the woodworking industry; flint, garnet, aluminum oxide and silicon carbide. The first two are natural abrasives and the last two are man-made.

Flint paper is probably the most familiar of all the abrasives sold in hardware stores across the country. It is an off-white color. Although it is sold everywhere, flint paper is really a poor choice for wood finishing because it is not as durable as other abrasives.

Garnet is harder than flint and therefore a better choice for sanding woodwork, especially finish sanding. It is reddish-brown in color and available in sheets, belts and disks.

Aluminum oxide is the third hardest abrasive available and is excellent for sanding hardwoods such as oak. Aluminum oxide is a by-product of aluminum ore, to which are added small amounts of other materials to create a brown colored abrasive that is fast cutting.

Silicon carbide is the hardest and sharpest of all the abrasives (you have heard of carbide sharpening stones) and is suitable for all types of sanding from rough work to final sanding. Silicon carbide is dark (almost black) in appearance and is generally considered softer than aluminum oxide while it is being used.

Abrasives for woodworking projects are available in 9 × 12 inch sheets for hand sanding, and smaller sheets for orbital or finish sanders, belts and disks. Generally speaking, if you have a portable or stationary sander you can find abrasive belts, disks or pads to fit it. Different grades of abrasives are used for different sanding jobs. The following table (Figure 9-1) lists the various uses for the different types of abrasives.

It is important to remember that you should work your way up to the smaller size grit abrasives as you get closer to the final finishing, from coarse to fine.

	Grit no.	Grade	General uses
Very fine	400 360 320 280 240 220	10/0 — 9/0 8/0 7/0 6/0	Polishing, finishing after stain, varnish or gloss paint has been applied. The last paper to be used.
Fine	180 150 120	5/0 4/0 3/0	For finish sanding prior to staining or sealing.
Medium	100 80 60	2/0 1/0 1/2	For final removal of rough texture.
Coarse	50 40 36	1 1 1/2 2	For sanding after rough sanding has been done.
Very coarse	30 24 20 16	2 1/2 3 3 1/2 4	For sanding very rough textured wood surfaces.

Figure 9-1: Table of grit sizes and intended uses.

If you have much sanding to do you should consider buying or renting some type of sanding machine, either a belt or finish type. Belt sanders are excellent for sanding plywood cabinets providing you use the sander correctly. Never allow the sander to remain in one spot for more than a few seconds or you may do damage to the finish veneer layer. Belt sanders are always used during finish work so that the belt rotation is the same as the grain of the wood. Sanding across the grain will remove a lot of wood quickly; keep this in mind if you have to fit or bevel some pieces. Sanding across the grain also leaves scratches on the face of the board and is therefore unsuitable for finish work. Whenever working with a belt sander keep the machine moving (with the grain) in a slow, even, flat motion. Never press down with all of your weight when sanding as this puts undue stress on the machine and work.

A finish sander should be used whenever the sanding is to be done lightly, e.g., between coats of paint or varnish.

It is important, regardless of the type of sander you are using, to choose the correct grade of paper for the piece you are working on. Refer back to the chart (Figure 9-1) for the different types of papers. Remember that sanding is designed to smooth and finish the surface after all cutting and shaping have been done with other tools. Careful sanding, preceded by careful cutting and assembly will insure that the finished cabinet lives up to your expectations.

For small sanding jobs you can use a small block of wood with abrasive paper attached or a small hand sander which is similar to a block with the addition of a felt pad between the paper and block. Even with a sanding block it is important to sand with the grain and to use the proper grit paper. Remember that it is a natural tendency to round off square edges when sanding— if edges are to be left square, keep this in mind while sanding (Figure 9-2).

Figure 9-2:   A hand block sander is useful for small sanding jobs.

Paint Brushes

It is a fallacy to think you can obtain a professional looking finish with an inexpensive paint brush. This is analogous to thinking that you can make clean, accurate wood cuts using a dull saw blade. Price is one indication of a quality paint brush but there are other guidelines that are equally important—bristle fibers, ferrule and handle.

A quality paint brush will have fibers that are either natural (commonly boar) or nylon. The bristles should feel full when squeezed between the fingers and the ends should be tapered so that when the brush is pressed on a flat surface a straight line is formed across the tips. Inexpensive brushes will feel full but when you press the fibers down on a flat surface, there will be an uneven bunch at the tips. With bristles such as these it is almost impossible to do accurate detail work (Figure 9-3).

The ferrule (metal junction between the bristles and handle) of a quality paint brush will be securely fastened to the handle of the brush. The handle itself can be either hardwood or plastic as long as it fits the hand well. A poorly designed handle leads to hand fatigue quickly and will result in a poor finishing job.

For just about every type of finish painting or varnishing project I prefer a brush commonly called a "varnish" or "enamel brush." This type of paint brush has a chisel edge to the bristles, and can be from 2- to 4-inches wide and ⅜- to 11/16-inches thick. A brush of this type is suitable for all plywood surfaces and will enable you to "flow" on several coats of either enamel or varnish.

It is interesting to note that commercial cabinet and counter makers spray on a finish coating using paint spraying equipment. You have to practice quite a number of hours with the equipment before you can expect to achieve a really professional looking painting job, and I feel that you can obtain just as good a finish using a quality paint brush.

For those readers interested in spray painting, you can rent the necessary equipment or you can buy a small compressor,

Figure 9-3: A quality paint brush will have tapered bristles enabling you to paint straight lines.

hoses, spray gun and attachments for about 50 dollars. Directions will be included for operation. All you will need is practice, practice, practice.

Finish Materials

Finish materials include fillers, sealers, primers, paints, clear finishes, stains, and waxes—surely something for everyone and a finish for any type of cabinet, counter, or vanity you could possibly build (Figure 9-4). In an effort to take some of the mystery out of finish coatings I will briefly discuss each of them.

Fillers are used as the first step in the finishing process for woods with large pores such as walnut, mahogany, oak, and ash. The purpose of a filler is to fill and level the pores of the wood and to add color (from slight to very dark) to the final finish. Proper application of a filler is more important than the finish coating for it is the filler which is the basis for the finish coat. Fillers are available in paste and liquid form. No filler is necessary for closed grained woods such as fir, pine, basswood, or poplar, but an application of a sealer is recommended.

Sealers for woods that have been filled (large pore woods) are necessary to prevent the filler from migrating into the finish

Figure 9-4: These are some of the possible choices for finishing cabinets, counters and vanities.

coat. Sealers are also a good idea for closed grain woods, especially plywood. Generally speaking, there are two types of sealers; shellac and synthetic resin. Shellac sealer is made by mixing one part four-pound-cut shellac (white) and seven parts alcohol. The shellac sealer is brushed on and allowed to dry before the finish coats are applied. Synthetic resin sealers are sold ready for use and are recommended for plywood cabinets. Synthetic sealers are applied in the same manner as shellac sealers, and help to prevent the wood from absorbing moisture. Sealers and fillers are used under clear finish coatings.

Primers are used when the finish coating will be paint. The main purpose of a primer is to prevent "bleeding" through of knots, nails, etc., and to provide a solid base for the finish coats. All previously unpainted wood which will ultimately be finished with water or oil base enamel should be primed with an enamel undercoat to seal the wood and provide a better under surface. If the unpainted cabinet is not primed, the enamel coat will be uneven. I prefer an oil base (exterior type) primer for all surfaces that will be receiving a finish of oil or water base paint. I have found that the oil base primers seem to penetrate the best and are the most dependable.

Generally speaking, the best choice of a solid color paint is one that is washable, and either gloss or semigloss. Paints with a flat finish texture are not recommended because they are not as easy to maintain. Even the inside of cabinets, counters and vanities should be given a coat of a gloss or semigloss paint. Enamels, including latex enamels, are preferred for the kitchen and bathroom because they withstand intensive cleaning and wear. These paints form especially hard films.

If the natural wood grain appearance of the cabinet is to be retained, you may want to consider using some type of wood stain to enhance and highlight the grain. Stains are available as water stain, oil stain, nongrain raising stains, and sealer stains.

Water stains are the least expensive of all the stains, and probably the simplest to use. These stains are sold as powders which you mix with hot water before using. The stain, when applied with a brush, is absorbed by the wood fibers, resulting in a stain that does not fade appreciably. On the negative side, water stains tend to swell the wood fibers and raise the grain. Most shades and colors are available.

Oil stains are sold as pigment or penetrating types. Pigment oil stains are best for wood surfaces with an uneven color as the stain will tend to even out the overall look. Pigment stains do not penetrate very deeply into the surface of the wood and can, therefore, be sanded off if desired. Penetrating oil stains are easier to apply than the pigmented types and, as the name suggests, actually penetrate into the wood. Both types of oil base stains are sold premixed in a variety of natural colors.

Nongrain raising stains are widely used in commercial work and are commonly sprayed on. They are excellent for cabinets which will be receiving a finish coat of varnish or other clear coating. These stains do not raise the grain of the wood and result in bright, transparent colors.

Sealer stains are another commercially popular stain as they perform two functions with one application. They are considered to be partly penetrating (sealing) and partly surface stains. The color of these stains is developed by adding drops of tinting color to a base liquid.

Varnishes form durable and attractive finishes for cabinets, counter fronts and vanities. They seal the wood forming tough, transparent films which will withstand frequent scrubbing and hard use, and are available in flat, semigloss (sometimes called satin) or high gloss finishes. Most varnishes, however, are easily scratched, and marks are difficult to conceal without redoing the entire surface. A good paste wax applied over the finished varnish, especially the fronts of cabinets and counters, will provide some protection against scratches.

Shellac and lacquer have uses similar to most varnishes, but these finishes are easy to repair or recoat. They apply easily, dry fast, and are also useful as a sealer and clear finish under varnish for all wood surfaces. The first coat should be thinned as recommended on the container, then sanded lightly and finished with one or more undiluted coats. Two coats will give a fair sheen, and three a high gloss.

Polyurethane and epoxy varnishes are noted for durability and high resistance to stains, abrasions, acids, strong cleaners, fuels, alcohol and many chemicals. Their toughness is the reason for the popularity of these clear finishes. They are easy to apply and repair. One point to remember, about polyurethane and epoxy varnishes, is that they will often develop a yellowish cast with age, which some people find objectionable.

Wax finishes can also be used as a protective finish coating on cabinets and counters. It is advisable, however, to first give the cabinet a few coats of shellac or other clear finish to provide a solid base for the wax. Paste or butcher type waxes are superior to liquid waxes from the standpoint of beauty and durability.

Waxes should be applied to wood surfaces with a soft cloth and rubbed with the grain. Follow manufacturer's instructions for application. If a wax surface becomes dirty with age, it can be cleaned with a mild household detergent, followed by a rinsing with a clean, damp cloth. Remember that a wax finish is not recommended if a different type of finish may be used later in the life of the piece, as wax is difficult to remove totally.

SURFACE PREPARATION

Surface preparation entails all of the operations that are necessary to prepare the cabinet, counter or vanity to the point where a finish coating can be applied. In most cases this will include filling ends of plywood doors, edges of drawers and exposed edges of the cabinet; sanding, sealing or filling, and painting the interiors of cabinets. As mentioned earlier in this chapter, the amount of energy you expend in preparing the surface will directly affect how the finished cabinet looks and endures. Some of these surface preparation tasks can be performed before installation, as in the case of small cabinets and bathroom vanities, while other surface preparation procedures must be done after the counter has been installed.

On some cabinets and counters built with plywood, you will have to do something with the exposed edges, i.e., around doors, drawers and exposed edges of the counter or cabinet. There are several edge treatment alternatives, two of which (covering with plastic laminate and edging material) are covered in Chapter 4, "Counter Tops." A third alternative involves filling the edge with either wood putty (a commercial sawdust and adhesive mixture) or your own mixture of white glue and sawdust from the lumber you have been working with, or plaster spackling material, commonly called joint compound. Whichever type of edge filling material you choose to use, the application will be about the same.

Begin by spreading the filler material along the edge with a putty knife or small spatula (Figure 9-5). It is important to force the filler into the end grain of the plywood so it will penetrate for a good bond. Care should be exercised so that you do not put this filler on too thick, just enough to make the edge appear (and in fact be) smooth. When this has dried, the edge should be sanded lightly to further create a smooth, flat, square edge.

It should be noted that spackle paste can be used effectively if the cabinet will be painted a solid color. If a clear finish is to be

(Courtesy of American Plywood Assn.)

Figure 9-5:   Careful filling of edges is essential for professional looking door edges.

used, or a stain and clear finish, you must do some experimenting to get the right color combinations. Wood putty will take a stain differently than the wood itself so close matching is difficult but not impossible. One way to overcome this is to use a dark stain which will mask the edge filler. The dark stain, will however, also make the grain of the wood almost unnoticeable. Whichever edge filler treatment you use remember that you want as light a coat as possible to do the job. Edges which have an excess of filler stand a good chance of cracking with age, especially doors which sometimes get slammed shut.

Cabinets and counters which have been dented or scratched can also be repaired with wood putty or spacke paste depending on how the cabinet will be finished, and providing the imperfection is only superficial. After the repair, the area should be sanded until the repaired area blends in with the area around it (Figure 9-6).

Pay close attention to the joint areas of the cabinet, and look for excess glue. Do not try to sand off excess glue, as this will force

(Courtesy of American Plywood Assn.)

Figure 9-6:   Dents and scratches should also be filled with wood putty or edge filler, then sanded flat when dry.

the glue into the pores of the wood, and in effect, cause the wood to be sealed. Always remove excess glue with a sharp knife or wood chisel (Figure 9-7).

The next step in surface preparation is to sand, sand, sand. Besides the edges and joints mentioned above, you will have to

Figure 9-7:   Excess glue should not be sanded off but removed with a sharp knife or wood chisel.

sand the body of the cabinet itself. Your goal should be to achieve as flat and smooth a surface as possible. You will able to do this by sanding with the grain and working with finer grades of abrasive paper until you are using extra-fine paper. You can use a hand sanding block for small areas, but you will find the work will go much quicker if you use an electric sander. In any event, the last sanding should be done by hand with a paper of about 180 grit. When all of the sanding has been completed, vacuum the surface to remove sanding dust.

Before painting, you might want to cover up certain areas, such as plastic laminate tops, which you do not want to receive a coat of paint. Newspaper and masking tape will make short work of this covering project.

Apply a filler, sealer or primer as required and discussed earlier in this chapter. You may recall that a filler is used on woods with large open pores, sealer is used on closed pore woods (especially plywood), and a primer is used on all wood surfaces which will receive a finish coat of paint.

If you will be staining the cabinet, this should be done after the filling, but before sealing. Consider using a stain that is both a stain and a sealer, as this will save some time and the results are about the same.

Before applying the final finish coat to the outside of the cabinet, you should have primed and applied the finish coat to the inside. Remember that the inside will be easier to wipe clean if the finish coating is either semigloss or high gloss enamel. Standard color is white for the inside of cabinets, as this will help to provide reflected light. Of course, you can paint the inside any color you want, but, generally speaking, lighter colors are best.

Before actually applying the finish coating, there are several things which you should be certain about. First, if you are applying a solid color paint, you should have applied some type of primer, filled all edges, nail holes, dents, etc., and the primer must be dry. All surfaces should be flat, level, and there should be no excess primer (this usually shows up as running globs). If the counter has any areas which are not in this condition, now is the time to correct them. Usually sanding (with a fine grit paper) will take care of this.

Secondly, you should make certain that the surface is free from dust, moisture, and anything else that may have an effect on the finish coat. You may find a tack cloth helpful before applying the final finish coat of either paint or clear finish. A tack cloth is simply a specially treated cloth—sold at all paint and hardware stores—which when wiped across a surface, will pick up any dust or loose dirt particles.

Lastly, you should use a clean, dry paintbrush for best results. Apply the finish coating with the grain, from the top of the cabinet toward the bottom (Figure 9-8). As you work, look at the paint job from different angles to make certain that the paint is not being applied too heavily in some areas, or that there are any loose brush bristles on the work. Excess paint can be brushed out over a large area. Stray bristles can be removed with the tip of the paint brush and your fingers. After you have applied the final coat of paint or clear finish, leave the area for a few hours to let the finish dry properly. Never work in an area where you have just applied the final finish coat as this will surely result in dust or dirt particles becoming airborne and coming to rest on the work.

After the cabinet has dried to a hard finish, look over the work. If the finish is clear, you may want to apply a paste wax for further protection and beauty. Although most paint manufacturers say that their paint will dry in eight hours, you should not use any freshly painted cabinet for at least 24 hours. This will insure the paint has had a chance to dry to a rock hard finish. Paint that has dried to the touch will mar if pressed into service at that time.

Figure 9-8: Always apply finish coat from the top of the piece downward, with the grain.

If you have conscientiously done all of the surface preparation work, applied appropriate fillers or sealers, sanded properly, and applied the finish coats (two or three) you can expect your new cabinet, counter or vanity to provide excellent service. The finish coating will protect the piece and keep it looking beautiful for many years.

CHAPTER 10

INSTALLATION

The final step of cabinet, counter or vanity building is installation and this part is as important as the construction or finishing steps. The finest cabinet you can build will be worthless if it is installed incorrectly; therefore, you must approach this stage of the work carefully. Another reason for careful installation work is that, in most cases the cabinet, counter or vanity will have been finished with some form of protective coating—clear finish, paint or plastic laminate—and you will not want to cause any damage to this coating.

With the exception of free standing counters or "islands," all cabinets, counters and vanities must be attached to the wall. In many cases it will be possible to attach the unit to both the floor and wall or, wall and ceiling for greater strength. Remember that just one shelf filled with canned goods can weight about 30 pounds, and if you have an entire cabinet filled with canned goods, you will have a total weight in the neighborhood of 125 pounds.

Therefore, it is easy to see that a cabinet must be securely fastened to the wall.

It may be helpful, before discussing cabinet installation to talk a bit about house framing and the 2 × 4 inch studs which make up the skeleton of most homes.

LOCATING WALL STUDS

Most modern building codes call for stud spacing of 16 inches on center. This means that the distance between the center of one stud to the center of the stud (left or right) will be 16 inches. Sometimes, however, especially in older houses, the studs will be spaced 24 inches on center. In any event, it is to the wall studs that cabinets, counters and vanities must be attached.

To find the existing wall studs, you simply measure 16 (or 24) inches from an existing wall or corner and tap lightly on the wall surface until you hear a solid sound. This will be a wall stud, and then, once you know the spacing between the studs, you will be able to mark their location and attach the cabinet.

Another way to locate wall studs is to look closely at the wall covering and try to find small dimples or indentations. These will be the dents of filled nail holes, for this is how dry walls are attached to the framing studs. The sheets are nailed into place, and the nail heads are driven just below the surface. These holes or dents are filled with joint compound (a form of plaster) to conceal the nail heads. With age, especially in humid areas of the country, these filled nail holes will sink slightly. Of course, this method of stud location can only be used if the existing finish wall covering consists of gypsum panels. If wood paneling or wallpaper is covering the wall, the nail hole coverings will be totally concealed by this covering.

If you are attaching a cabinet to a ceiling (or wall and ceiling) you can find the ceiling joists in the same manner as you found the wall studs. First, however, you must determine the direction of the joists, then the spacing.

Masonry Attachment

Some homes have concrete, cinder block or brick walls and no framing or wall studs whatsoever. For walls of this type, you will have to use masonry fasteners to hold the cabinet to the wall. Another possibility, when masonry walls are present, is to attach

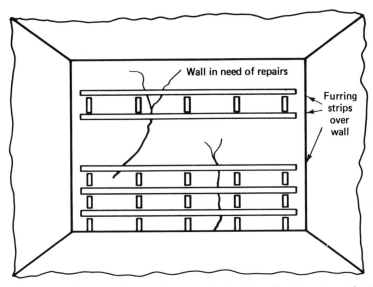

Figure 10-1: For problem walls it may be best to attach furring strips to the studs (over the wall covering) then attach the cabinets to these strips.

furring strips (1 × 2 inch lumber) or studs to the wall surface, then attach the cabinets to these (see Figure 10-1).

The simplest, and least expensive frame to attach to a masonry wall is the one constructed from 1 × 2 inch furring strips. Simply attach the furring strips horizontally, the full length of the wall, spaced 2 feet apart. The strips are attached to the masonry wall with masonry fasteners.

Masonry fasteners, in case you are not familiar with them, are of several different types. Probably the strongest masonry fastener is called a lead anchor (Figure 10-2) and this is universally

Figure 10-2: A lead wall anchor is used for attaching cabinets to masonry walls.

available. To install a lead anchor you must first mark the location of where you want it to be, then drill a hole in the masonry wall. The hole can be easily bored with a carbide tipped drill bit in an electric drill. The hole should be just slightly larger than the lead anchor diameter and deeper than the lead anchor is long. While drilling the lead anchor holes, you must keep the drill and bit at a 90 degree angle to the face of the wall or the resultant hole will be at the wrong angle and result in a poor installation. You should also wear some type of eye protection when drilling masonry as the dust (which is actually cement powder) is an eye irritant.

After the hole has been bored, you can insert the lead anchor. Then, when all of the holes have been drilled and the lead anchors inserted, you can attach the furring strips. The bolts are pushed through holes in the furring strip and screwed into the lead anchors in the masonry wall. As each bolt is turned into its lead anchor, the anchor will expand and hold itself firmly to the masonry wall. When you have securely attached the required number of furring strips to the face of the masonry wall, you can then attach the cabinets to these. The resultant gap between the back of the cabinet and the wall under the cabinet is covered with suitable quarter-round molding.

Another way to fasten the strips to the wall is with a rented nail gun. This tool drives a nail into concrete by using an explosive charge (similar to a blank .22 caliber bullet). Nail guns are very effective for this type of work.

ATTACHING CABINETS

As mentioned earlier in this chapter, most American homes have walls with 2 × 4 inch studs, covered with some type of finish wall covering (in most cases gypsum panels). There are several ways which you can attach wall hung cabinets to walls of this type. You can attach the cabinets directly to the wall studs, to some type of bridging, which was first securely fastened to the existing wall studs, or you can attach the cabinets to the finish wall covering (providing the existing wall covering is in sound condition and can hold the weight of the cabinets).

If you plan to attach your cabinet, counter or vanity directly to the wall studs, you must first determine the stud location as explained above. Then, position the cabinet against the wall, noting the location of the studs, and then drill holes through the

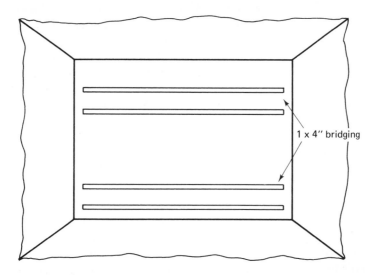

1 x 4" bridging

Figure 10-3:   Bridging, using 1 × 4 inch boards, provides a very strong base for attaching cabinets to walls.

cabinet back and into the wall studs. You should attach the cabinet using long wood screws that will pass through the cabinet backwall covering and at least one inch into the studs. In most cases these screws will be about 2½ inches long. Countersink the heads of these screws.

Another method of attaching cabinets to the wall studs involves the use of a bridge between the studs (Figure 10-3). After the location of the studs has been determined, as well as the location of the cabinets, you can attach either furring strips or 1 × 4 inch lumber across the face of the wall. Usually two pieces of lumber will suffice, one about 8 inches down from the location of the top of the cabinet and another about one foot up from the bottom of the cabinet.

The furring strips or 1 × 4s can be nailed through the finish wall covering and into the studs or, for added strength, they can be attached with large wood screws or lag bolts. After the wooden bridging has been attached to the finished wall, the cabinets are attached to the bridging with suitable length wood screws.

The bridging method of cabinet installation provides a very strong base for wall hung cabinets and can be used with cabinets that have either a solid back or partial back. If the cabinets you are installing have only a partial back, however, you must install the bridging at the exact location of the cabinet back strips.

If the existing wall on which you are installing cabinets is in bad shape with cracks, bulges, or other damage, the bridging method may be the simplest way to install the cabinets. The bridging will, in fact, provide a level surface on which you can attach the cabinets and eliminate the need for extensive repair work to the wall. If however, while attaching the bridging over the wall in need of repair, you find that the wall crumbles excessively, it may be best to remove the existing finish wall covering and re-cover the entire wall with a new wall covering, and then install the cabinets.

Direct Attachment

The last method we will discuss for attaching counters, cabinets and vanities to a wall is the direct attachment method. Here the cabinets are attached directly to the finish wall covering, using hollow wall fasteners (Figure 10-4) to hold the cabinet in place. This method can be used for old plaster and lath walls or the more modern gypsum or dry walls, but keep in mind that this is not the strongest method of cabinet attachment. It is suitable, however, for counters and vanities which sit on the floor.

Begin by determining the location of the cabinet on the wall. Next, holes are drilled through the plaster and into the hollow space inside the wall. These holes must be large enough to accommodate either toggle bolts or expansion fasteners (commonly

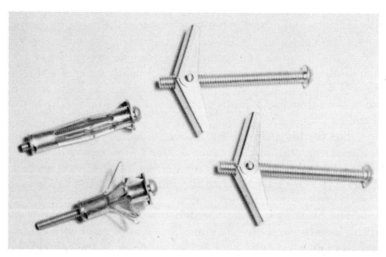

Figure 10-4:   Molly's (left) and toggle bolts (right) can be used to hang cabinets on hollow walls.

called "molly's"). Since toggle bolts and molly's are attached in a slightly different manner I will discuss each separately.

A toggle bolt (which can also be used for hollow concrete walls) is simply a long bolt with a pair of foldable wings which serve at the nut. First, a hole large enough for the folded wings to pass through is drilled in the hollow wall, at the location of the cabinet fastening point. Then the bolt of the toggle bolt is inserted through the cabinet back and the wings attached to the end of the bolt. Next, the cabinet is positioned on the wall, the wings of the toggle are folded and passed through the hole in the wall and into the hollow space. As the toggle bolt passes into the open space, the wings open and cannot be removed. The bolt is turned until the cabinet is pulled up tight against the wall surface. Toggle bolts are a very strong method of cabinet attachment but are meant for permanent installations and where the necessary holes will be covered by the cabinet.

Toggle bolts are available in many different sizes but you must remember that they cannot possibly hold up cabinets if the existing wall in in bad shape.

Molly's can be attached in two ways; either driven into the wall or pushed through a predrilled hole. After installation, however, all molly's work in the same way. The screw is turned until you feel a lot of resistance; the molly sleeve is mushrooming against the back of the wall. Once you feel the molly has totally expanded, you remove the screw, pass it through the cabinet back and then screw it into the expanded molly sleeve in the wall. Molly's are available in several different sizes but, as with toggle bolts, should not be used to hold cabinets on walls that are not sound.

Of the two types of hollow wall fasteners, the toggle is the strongest. The molly should be used only when the cabinet weight will not be excessive or when the unit rests on the floor.

Floor Installation

So far we have discussed the various methods of attaching cabinets to walls—either to the existing studs, bridging, or directly to the finished wall. Of course, counters and vanities are attached to the floor as well as the wall. In many instances the floor will not be level and you will have to make an adjustment or two so that the final installation will result in a counter that is level. There are two ways of installing a cabinet on an uneven surface so that the finished cabinet is level: using shims or cutting the bottom of the cabinet.

The shim method begins by positioning the cabinet against the wall at its intended location. Next, set a level on top of the cabinet to determine how much the cabinet is out of level. Then tap pieces of cedar shingles (these are tapered) under the cabinet bottom until the bubble in the level is in the center. Because the cedar shingles are tapered, they raise the cabinet as they are driven under the cabinet bottom As you tap the shingle under the cabinet, keep an eye on the level and when the cabinet is plumb, attach the cabinet to the wall, using one of the previously discussed methods, until it is securely fastened. The next step is to remove those parts of the cedar shingle shims which protrude from the cabinet bottom. This is most easily done with a sharp chisel and mallet (Figure 10-5). The space between the cabinet bottom and the floor is covered with molding.

As a side note, I will mention that the shim method of cabinet installation is the method most often used to install ready-made cabinets. In fact, these units come with a package of cedar shingles or wedges, which are used for the shimming.

The second method of installing a cabinet or counter involves cutting the bottom of the cabinet so that the top will be level, while the base sits on the floor. Begin by positioning the cabinet against the wall in the location you want it to be installed. Then, using a level, determine the finished position of the cabinet. Next, you must measure the distance the cabinet is out of level; temporary shims or blocks may be helpful to hold the cabinet in position while you measure. Then the amount the cabinet is out must be removed from the opposite end of the cabinet bottom.

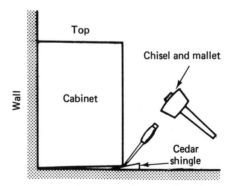

Figure 10-5: After the cabinet has been leveled by tapping a piece of cedar shingle under the base, the excess shingle is removed with a chisel and mallet.

In most cases floors slope away from the wall. This will mean that you will have to remove a predetermined amount on each side of the cabinet so that when the trimmed cabinet is set up against the wall, the top will be level and plumb (Figure 10-6).

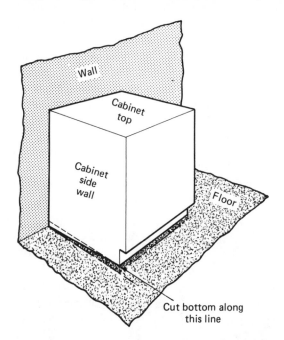

Figure 10-6:   To make a cabinet sit level on an unlevel floor it may be necessary to remove a predetermined part of the cabinet bottom.

Accuracy in measuring and cutting cannot be overemphasized for this method of cabinet installation, and the old carpenter's rule of "measure twice, cut once" will be helpful.

After the cabinet base has been trimmed, the cabinet is repositioned against the wall, then checked with a level. If the top is level, you can attach the cabinet to the wall using one of the previously discussed methods. The bottom of the cabinet, where it sits on the floor, is covered with a suitable molding for a final finished appearance.

If you are attaching more than one cabinet to the surface of a wall you must, in addition to securing the cabinet to the wall, fasten the cabinets themselves together. This is most easily accomplished by screwing the sides of the adjoining cabinets together after each has been attached properly to the wall.

The order of installation of kitchen counter and cabinets is obvious. First you install the counter base units to the wall, then the counter top. After you are satisfied with the counter, you can install the wall hung cabinets. Remember that the distance between the top of the counter and the bottom of the wall hung cabinet is important and you should plan thoroughly as well as thoughtfully. (Refer to Chapter 2, Figure 2-5.)

The wall area between the top of the counter and the bottom of the wall hung cabinet (often called the back splash area) should be finished in some manner after the installation of the storage units. The possibilities include installing ceramic tile or wood paneling or simply painting the area in a suitable color with gloss or semigloss paint (Figure 10-7).

The area above the tops of wall hung cabinets can be treated in two ways. This space can be left as is and used for storage of various types of kitchen equipment or, a drop or false ceiling can be built over the top of the cabinet (Figure 10-8).

(Courtesy of Tile Council of America)

Figure 10-7:   The area between the top of the counter and the bottom of the wall hung cabinets can be covered with tile for an effective and attractive back splash area.

(Courtesy of Tile Council of America)

Figure 10-8:   The area above the wall hung cabinets can be left open, as in this photo, or a false ceiling can be constructed.

To build a drop ceiling, you must first frame out the area above the cabinets. This can usually be done with 2 × 3 inch lumber, spaced 24 inches on center. Once the frame work has been constructed, it can be covered with gypsum panels and then suitably finished.

An alternative to the dry wall drop ceiling over the tops of wall hung cabinets is to build a suitable frame and cover it with some type of attractive wood paneling. Of course, if you build a drop ceiling over the cabinet you will not have the additional storage space that is available when the top of the cabinet is left open.

Installing cabinets is not difficult, but you should devote enough careful work and energy to insure that the finished job looks finished. Once properly installed, kitchen counters, cabinets, and bathroom vanities should provide years of solid well hung service.

Index